Explore
TASMANIA

Jennifer Pringle-Jones

**Publishing House
of Tasmania Pty Ltd**

This is the second edition of **Explore Tasmania** by journalist/researcher Jennifer Pringle-Jones, whose other books include **Tasmania is a Garden** and **Discovering Tasmania.** Perhaps best known as a Logie-winning television and current affairs reporter, Jennifer worked more recently as Communications Officer with the Commonwealth Scientific and Industrial Research Organisation in Hobart. Her special interest is travel writing, and she is a regular contributor to national and international publications, such as Fodor's Guide to Australia, New Zealand and the South Pacific.

Cover: Richmond, Tasmania.

Photo: Thor Carter

Author : Jennifer Pringle-Jones

Publisher: Publishing House of Tasmania Pty Ltd

Distributor: Book Agencies of Tasmania
          65 Maluka Street Bellerive Tasmania
          (002) 443177

Book design : Bruce W. Irving
Photographs : Robert Cartmel Bruce W. Irving
Typesetting : Creative Typographics Pty Ltd

Printed in Hong Kong

Acknowledgements:
Archives Office of Tasmania
Auto Rent/Budget
Department of Tourism
Government Photographic Section
Hydro Electric Commission
Innkeepers Motor Inns
Lands Department for maps
National Parks & Wildlife Service

CSIRO
Thor Carter

National Library of Australia Cataloguing-in-Publication data
Pringle-Jones, Jennifer 1946 –
Explore Tasmania
Includes index
ISBN 1 875210 01 6
1. Tasmania — Description and travel — 1976 —
I. Title
919 46'0463

Contents

INDIAN
OCEAN

PACIFIC
OCEAN

TASMANIA

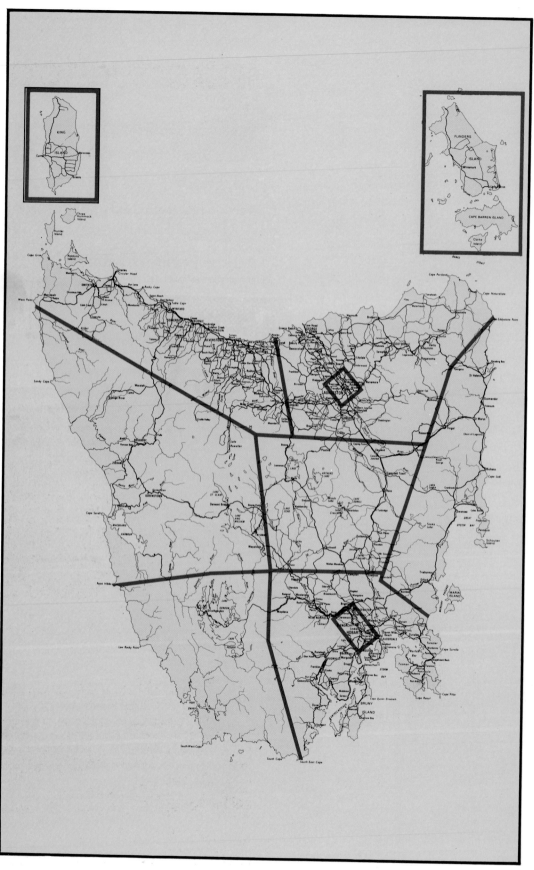

Introduction

In three centuries the small island of Tasmania has changed from a mysterious land of unknown splendour, to a place in the full focus of world attention.

In 1642 the Dutch navigator Abel Janszoon Tasman became the first European to see this mountainous land but he was never to learn its innermost secrets. They were known only to a nomadic brown-skinned people whose ancestors probably came to the area more than 18,000 years before. At that stage the land was joined to the rest of the Australian land mass but, when the world's ice cap thawed about 11,000 years ago, a 240 km strait developed, cutting off this southern section. Tasman named the island "Van Diemen's Land" after the Governor of Batavia, Anthony Van Diemen, who had commissioned the voyage.

The Tasmanian Aborigines lived on shellfish, vegetable foods such as seaweed and native potatoes, birds' eggs and meat from wallabies, wombats and Tasmanian devils. They used spears and stone tools like their counterparts in other areas of Australia, but didn't have spear throwers, boomerangs, shields or axes.

However, it was 130 years after Tasman's discovery before other adventurers delved into this "treasure trove", their ships driven by the roaring forties — winds which blow from west to east along the 40th Parallel of latitude. Frenchmen were followed by Englishmen and, eventually, fear that the French might lay claim to the area prompted British authorities in the colony of New South Wales to send an expedition to Van Diemen's Land to secure it for the Crown.

The first settlements were at Risdon Cove in 1803 and, soon afterwards, at York Town in the North. The Risdon Cove settlement was soon abandoned in favour of a site on the western shore of the Derwent River where Hobart Town developed into what is now the City of Hobart and the State capital; the York Town settlement was also abandoned in favour of Launceston, the State's second city.

At the time of European settlement in Van Diemen's Land there were probably about 2,000 Aborigines, but by 1830 the number had dwindled to 200 and the last full-blooded Tasmanian Aborigine died in 1876.

For generations explorers sailed the seas in search of riches and new lands. Tasman found both here, and his achievement was honoured in 1856 by changing the island's name to Tasmania.

Left: Aborigines — Tasmania's first settlers.
Top: Hobart wharves — a mecca for 19th and 20th century visitors.
Bottom: Launceston dominated by a colonial hospital 1867.

The first 50 years saw an initial battle for sheer survival followed by exploration, advances in agriculture and trade ... but the penal system was the backdrop to it all. Many of the 74,000 convicts whose destiny led them to Van Diemen's Land contributed to development of the colony in areas as diverse as the Arts (such as artist Thomas Bock) and construction work (architects James Blackburn and William Archer, and sculptor James Herbert whose famous carvings on the Ross Bridge make this the most architecturally important bridge in Australia).

The Victorian Gallery, showpiece of the Tasmanian Museum and Art Gallery.

The Ross bridge is an architectural gem.

Tasmania has had a number of Australian firsts (public library, novel, trunk telephone line and even compulsory education), but probably its greatest attribute is its fine quality of life. Even its much-maligned climate is actually "temperate maritime" in type and compares more than favourably with centres on the Mediterranean.

Distinct geographical differences within the 68,000 square kilometres of Tasmania (rugged mountain ranges, highland lakes, coastal plains and dense wilderness) governed regional development; patterns established in the 19th century pioneering days are reflected in present times.

Picturesque Hobart from the docks.

Early travellers came in sailing ships, but today Tasmania is serviced by a vehicular ferry which makes crossings three times weekly from Devonport to Melbourne; by several daily air services which connect Hobart, Launceston, Devonport and Wynyard with Melbourne and Sydney; and by flights between Hobart and New Zealand, plus international Qantas connections. Intrastate carriers service major centres, including King and Flinders Islands (also serviced from Victoria). Within the State it's possible to hire virtually any form of transport — from donkeys to campervans, windsurfers to cabin cruisers, bicycles to light planes.

Evandale, an historic village.

Mt King William is typical of Tasmania's majestic peaks.

Lush farmlands near Boat Harbour, North-West Coast. Basalt soils extend right to the coast as vivid green gives way to deep blue.

Most people travel by road, so that is how we shall start, but there will be plenty of detours for unexpected pleasures, such as "encounters" with 20th century Tasmanians who recall many of the anecdotes and events which helped to shape the island we find today ...

Top: Hobart from the waterfront.
Bottom: Victoria Dock and Hobart Sheraton Hotel.

Hobart

Hobart, Australia's second oldest city, has managed to combine the benefits of a modern city with a feeling for the past; it has a rich heritage of buildings dating from the early years of settlement.

Hobart's life has always been centred on the magnificent Derwent estuary, one of the world's finest deepwater harbours. In 1803 a party of soldiers, settlers and convicts under the command of Lieutenant John Bowen settled at Risdon Cove. But, when Lieutenant-Colonel David Collins sailed to the Derwent estuary just five months later, he decided the original site was unsuitable because it lacked fresh water and so founded a second settlement further downstream. The tiny settlement was named after Lord Hobart, Secretary of State for the Colonies. Just over 300 people established a village that steadily extended along both sides of the river and up the surrounding hills; today more than 170,000 people live in the Greater Hobart area.

Hobart Town was initially a port for landing free settlers, convicts and their supplies, but it was soon exploited as a base for South Sea whalers ...

On Good Friday 1847 there were 47 whalers, both local and foreign, re-fitting and re-victualling in the Hobart port. Associated activities such as cooperage and shipbuilding flourished, but by the 1880s whale oil was being replaced by other fuels and the boom in the whaling industry had ended. Many early merchants made their fortunes in this trade; the last whaling voyage out of Hobart in 1899 marked the end of an era.

Hobart's development was based on trade and commerce. Early exports included corn and Merino wool, and the establishment of the centre as a free port boosted business, especially the Sydney wheat trade.

One of Australia's great industrial empires — the IXL jam and fruit processing works — was founded in Hobart by Henry Jones, whose name still is seen on buildings which "guard" the original wharf area ...

It used to be quite bare around the wharves earlier this century, according to Mrs Jessie Walker. She was born in 1897 and in her youth would call on her father at his office. He was Secretary of the Hobart Gas Company, which had premises at the bottom of Macquarie Street — a key area now in the extensive development of the Sullivan's Cove area.

Most people walked everywhere, but the advent of double-decker trams changed all that. Later single trams were also introduced and an Australian "first" — electrically powered trolley buses.

One trip favoured by tram users was out to Lenah Valley (then called Kangaroo Valley) for gooseberry-picking. Mrs Walker lived "en route" at New Town and used to watch the pickers alight from trams at the bottom of Augusta Road and walk to the Valley. The product of the days picking was sold to Jones and Co., and provided a valuable source of pocket money.

Most of Hobart's family businesses, which were a feature of commerce in Mrs Walker's youth, have been taken over by big companies — or disappeared altogether. Visits to Arnold's Cake Shop, established in 1854 and run by three generations of the Arnold family, were special occasions.

Mrs Walker's earliest memories are of visits each Sunday to her grandfather, who lived at Bellerive. These trips also had the bonus of a ferry boat ride — and the harbour itself, always was full of activity ...

Cascades was among suburbs served by Hobart's trams until the 1960's.

No storms in this port

Port activities today concentrate on the shipment of newsprint, timber, fruit and general cargo, and, during the Christmas-New Year period, the port is a focal point for activities associated with the Sydney to Hobart Yacht Race and the Westcoaster Yacht Race from Victoria to Hobart. The Sydney to Hobart Race is one of the world's classic yachting events, comparable to the Fastnet and Bermuda Races. During the two weeks after Christmas Day, Hobart displays a festival atmosphere, hosting open air concerts, art shows and sporting events, many of them centred on the waterfront.

Another annual highlight is the Royal Hobart Regatta; started in 1838 and held each February, it is the largest aquatic carnival in the southern hemisphere.

A wealth of things to see and do

Nestling at the foot of Mt Wellington (1,271 m), Hobart is one of the world's most picturesque cities. It offers a full range of accommodation, shopping and sporting amenities, cultural and convention facilities ... and history "at every corner".

These days it's rare to find streets lined with sandstone buildings, but some parts of Hobart could belong to last century.

Macquarie Street has more than 30 buildings classified by the National Trust including the Town Hall (built on the site where Collins proclaimed the capital), St David's Cathedral, Government and private offices and clubs.

Still a business centre

On the waterfront the row of Georgian sandstone warehouses in Salamanca Place is an unequalled example of Australian colonial architecture. The buildings were the centre for trade and commerce from the 1830s and now form a focal point for businesses selling items ranging from vegetables to antiques, and art and crafts of all kinds. A highlight each week is the Saturday morning market when stalls cover the roads and pavements and people browse in the numerous stores along laneways and in the warehouse complex itself.

During the week Salamanca Place is a base for numerous craftsmen while a little farther along, in Castray Esplanade, there's headquarters of another kind — the CSIRO Marine Laboratories.

The Salamanca Arts Festival is held towards the end of the year, providing workshops and displays for all tastes, while restaurants and inns provide fare for the "inner self".

Parliament and parks

Also on the waterfront, and adjoining Salamanca Place, is Tasmania's Parliament House. Originally the Customs House and Bond Store, it became the seat of the Parliament when the colony was granted self-government in 1856. Tasmania has a House of Assembly (the Lower House) and a Legislative Council (the Upper House).

Parliament House grounds provide a pleasant resting spot, while nearby St David's Park is a resting ground of another kind. This was the original burial ground for Hobart and some of the old headstones have been erected in a memorial wall.

Battery Point — maritime links

Kelly's Steps in Salamanca Place are a quaint reminder of the days when they provided a handy link for mariners between the waterfront and their Battery Point homes. The Steps were built on land believed to have belonged to Captain James Kelly, one of the first important Australian-born mariners. He later became harbourmaster and one of the many seafaring people who settled in the maritime village of Battery Point.

In 1852 the list of residents included master mariners, merchants, shipwrights, coopers, seamen and fishermen, and their homes reflect their different lifestyles. Rows of conjoined cottages in Battery Point contrast with the Italienate style mansion, Lenna, now a hotel and restaurant.

Sandstone buildings are a feature of the Hobart city area.

There's something for everyone at the market in Salamanca Place.

The area also has colonial accommodation, historic hotels such as the Shipwright's Arms, coffee houses, antique shops and specialist restaurants — Mure's Fish House; Dirty Dick's Steak House; Sakura (Japanese); Salamanca Terrace; Ball and Chain Grill; Rockefellers, in an original waterfront inn, and Dear Friends. Right on the waterfront there are the Gazebo and Sullivans in the Hobart Sheraton, Mure's Dockside Fish Centre, and the Drunken Admiral.

Battery Point has many art and craft galleries, a shop featuring woven and knitted goods, and a folk museum. Visitors can spend hours wandering around Battery Point's streets and laneways, but, on guided tours conducted by the National Trust, it is also possible to explore underground chambers built to store ammunition and supplies for the Mulgrave

Battery, (details from the Trust, which also runs a delightful gift shop in architecturally interesting Galleria development).

Other features near the park include the signal station, once a guard house and now the oldest building in Battery Point, and, at the foot of the former harbourmaster's garden, a tiny octagonal building which is the base for all distance measurement in Tasmania.

Arthur's Circus, with its 16 plots radiating from a circular road, has a quaint collection of cottages dating to the middle of last century. There is a touch of yesteryear, too, in the lamp post at the centre of the green.

Battery Point, with its central landmark, St George's Church, still retains its village atmosphere and reminders of the past which have been carefully retained for future generations.

Modern attractions as well

No city can live on history alone, and Hobart's best known modern attraction, the Wrest Point Hotel-Casino in Sandy Bay, was Australia's first legal gambling centre of this type.

Thousands of people from all over the world try their luck at the tables or playing two-up (a traditional Australian game involving coin-tossing) or keno (a computerised lottery). Restaurants and a cabaret room cater for all tastes in dining, a revolving restaurant on the 17th floor of the tower block offering superb views during its one hour circuit.

Other features include a discotheque and extensive convention facilities in a waterfront complex.

In the heart of the city, there is a new multi-storey international hotel — the Hobart Sheraton. In a superb dockside setting, it has informal and formal dining rooms, an atrium bar, where guests can watch boating activities while listening to background piano music, a convention centre, pool, sauna and spa. Suites have views to the harbour or Mt Wellington.

Cottages and mansions ... Battery Point has them all.

Blackjack is popular "at the tables".

The Wrest Point Hotel-Casino is a glittering spectacle.

Botanical gardens — a quiet oasis

The Royal Tasmanian Botanical Gardens on the Queen's Domain next to Government House (not open to the public) have combined the gardens and parklands with some less traditional attractions. A Huon Pine sculpture was erected to mark the 200th anniversary of the beginning of French exploration and scientific discovery in Tasmanian waters, and there is an unusual shelter made from Tasmanian oak and celery top pine with the even more unusual name of Wombat One. The home of early superintendents of the Gardens is now a museum and education centre: Huon Pine, Tasmanian scents, bees and honey production are just a few of the subjects presented in the displays. The 280 m long Eardley Wilmot Wall between the gardens and Government House, is believed to be the longest convict-built brick wall still standing. The conservatory, one of the best in the Commonwealth, and a recently established Japanese garden, complete with miniature Mt. Fuji, are among special attractions at the gardens, which are open daily. There's a kiosk and restaurant, too.

Museums of all types

Hobart has a wide variety of museums, and at the Tasmanian Museum and Art Gallery in Macquarie Street even the buildings themselves are museum pieces! Hobart's oldest building, the Commissariat Store established in 1808, now forms part of the museum complex. The Art Gallery houses one of Australia's most representative collections of colonial art, watercolours and prints.

Among other features are the Aboriginal displays and whaling and shipping exhibits, including a 1797 cannon salvaged from the bed of Sullivan's Cove — just a stone's throw from the Museum. A $2 million coin collection has examples from the earliest system of barter to the present decimal currency.

The Museum opens daily except Christmas Day, Good Friday and Anzac Day.

Keeping in touch with the past

The Allport Museum and Library of Fine Arts in the State Library building in Murray Street, houses a fine collection of art, furniture, silver and china. It was created by the bequest of the late Henry Allport, a Hobart solicitor, whose ancestors arrived in Tasmania in 1831. The collection is open between 9 a.m. and 5 p.m. each week day, except for public holiays.

Old lace and nursery items are just a few exhibits at Narryna, an historic building with interesting outhouses. Known as the Van Diemen's Land Memorial Folk Museum, it is in Hampden Road, Battery Point, and reflects social lifestyles of the 19th century.

In contrast, there are tours three times daily of the old Penitentiary Chapel and Criminal Courts, including underground cells, on the corner of Brisbane and Campbell Streets. This is now the headquarters of the National Trust.

Royal Tasmanian Botanical Gardens conservatory.

An Australian "first"

The Lady Franklin Museum at Lenah Valley was the first public museum in Australia. The 1843 Grecian-style building was built on the initiative of Lady Jane Franklin, wife of the Tasmanian Governor, who wanted Hobart to be the "Athens of the South"

The Post office Museum and Philatelic Sales Centre in Castray Esplanade (by the red post box!) has displays illustrating the development of post and telegraph services in Tasmania. It's also possible to climb the tower of the G.P.O. on the corner of Elizabeth and Macquarie Streets to see something more of postal "workings" (details from Australia Post).

Other special collections include a Transport Museum at Glenorchy, a Maritime Museum in historic Secheron House in Battery Point. The Maritime Museum is open between 1 p.m. and 4.30 p.m. and has photographs, paintings, marine equipment and an extensive model collection.

Classics — and classic photos

The John Elliott Classics Museum is at the University of Tasmania in Sandy Bay, while Beatties Historic Photo Museum in Cat and Fiddle Arcade (near a famous animated nursery rhyme clock) has a superb photographic record of Tasmania's history (copies of photos are on sale).

National Trust home

The National Trust is very active throughout Tasmania. It now owns Runnymede, a Regency-style home built in the 1840s in Bay Road, New Town. Originally called Bishopstowe, its previous occupants included a bishop, shipowner and lawyer. Furnishings are in keeping with the 19th century and it's possible also to inspect the grounds, coach house and stables.

Churches hold fascination

Hobart has a number of interesting churches.

St David's Cathedral in Macquarie Street (noted for its carved screen and stained glass windows) has a collection of stones from many of England's famous abbeys and cathedrals.

St George's Church in Battery Point is known as the Mariners' Church. It is built in the Greek Revival style and adjoining it is one of Tasmania's first schoolhouses.

Holy Trinity Church in North Hobart has a special connection with Hobart Regattas. It has the oldest peal of bells in Australia and they were first rung in 1847 to usher in Regatta Day. The bells were restored in Britain as a Bicentennial gift to Australia.

Anglesea Barracks — military base

This is the oldest military establishment in Australia still occupied by the Army. In the grounds, reached from Davey Street, there are restored buildings, including a museum featuring military records, uniforms and decorations.

In the grounds there are two imposing wheel-mounted bronze cannons. One theory suggests that they were souvenired from the brig H.M.S. Sirius by a detachment of the 73rd Regiment which served in Hobart for four years

from 1810. A modern monument, a fountain made from the stone of buildings destroyed in massive bushfires in southern Tasmania in 1967, commemorates the assistance of both regular and citizen soldiers during the disaster.

An ancient game

Royal tennis originated in France and, in the mid 14th century, it became popular in England. Hobart has one of only two royal tennis courts in Australia, and it's now more than 100 years old. The game is played in fascinating stone buildings opposite St David's Park in Davey Street.

Theatre with ghostly stories!

The Theatre Royal in Campbell Street was built in 1834 for £2,300 and originally was called the Royal Victoria. Performers have included Sir Harry Lauder, Lord Olivier and Noel Coward. Rumour has it that "Fred the Ghost" still lurks in The Shades, formerly a basement drinking house.

This is Australia's oldest surviving theatre — even a massive fire in 1984 failed to eliminate this architectural gem from the theatrical scene.

It was built by Peter Degraves, who also designed and built the Cascade Brewery, his architectural skills being developed while in gaol for non-payment of a debt! The original brewery was erected in 1824 at the base of Mt Wellington, and it was re-built in 1927.

Morning tours are held Monday to Thursday.

History has been preserved at Anglesea Barracks.

A bird's eye view

With its many hills Hobart can always be viewed "from above", but the two most popular vantage points are at Mt Wellington and Mt Nelson.

The road to Mt Wellington (1,271 m) opened in 1937, its construction providing vital employment during the Depression. There are lookouts and shelters at several points and the panoramic view from the summit is regarded as one of the finest in the world.

The mountain, which protects Hobart from prevailing westerly winds, often carries a mantle of snow in the winter and, when falls are heavy, access to the pinnacle is restricted. Walking tracks in the mountain reserve include a 3 km route from the Springs to the pinnacle, past a rock formation called the Organ Pipes, and the Zig Zag track — true to its name! Refreshments can be obtained at Fern Tree, the mountain access point.

Mt Nelson — signal point

Mt Nelson signal station was responsible for notifying Hobart Town of the imminent arrival of ships by flying the vessel's flag from the station mast. It also served as a link in the semaphore system of relaying messages from Port Arthur.

There are tearooms at the summit and a walking track leads through Trugannini Park to Taroona.

A sight to remember.

Panoramic view from Mount Nelson.

Hobart is the starting point for a number of specialised tours ...

- National Trust walking tours of Battery Point start in Franklin Square at 9.30 a.m. each Saturday, or at other times by arrangement.

- Harbour and Derwent River cruises operate throughout the year from the wharf, and refreshments are available on board.

- The **Cartela** and **Commodore I** have day and evening cruises, while the **Derwent Explorer** also carries passengers to Kettering in the D'Entrecasteaux Channel.

- Commuter ferry trips are made at regular intervals throughout the day between Hobart and Bellerive.

- For a nominal sum the Metropolitan Transport Trust issues daily off-peak zone tickets, and passengers can hop on and off buses journeying as far as Mt Nelson, Opposum Bay, Seven Mile Beach (recreation area), Fern Tree or Brighton.

- Helicopters and light planes can be chartered at Cambridge. Tasair and Par Avion flights include ones over the city and Derwent estuary, to the Tasman Peninsula, Lake Pedder (via the Derwent Valley and Arthur Range), south-west to Port Davey (landing strip) and Bathurst Harbour, and to Maria Island, landing near Darlington. Par Avion can combine flights with Wilderness Tours around Bathurst Harbour.

- Golden Arrow tour guides are simple to follow. Brochures from the Town Hall in Macquarie Street guide motorists through routes with signposted golden arrows around the city and environs.

- Tagalong Tours in mini-coaches collect patrons from their motels for trips close to Hobart.

- Bushventures four-wheel drive day tours travel south to the Huon, through magnificent forests and on to the Tahune Forest Reserve and Hartz Mountains; west to the Styx River and Florentine Valleys, and to world heritage areas, including the Franklin River.

- Open Spaces offer a variety of kayaking and rafting excursions from 1-16 days' duration.

- Under 30s are catered for by the Camping Connection in camping/hotel tours ranging from 7 to 14 days. They operate between November and May, and even the driver and cook are under 30!.

- Wilderness Tours have a variety of holidays (hiking and camping) in the south-west, while other specialised interests which are catered for include deep sea fishing, trout fishing and golf.

Details of all these are available from Tasmanian Travel Centres.

Franklin Square and government buildings.

Glenorchy — a city in its own right

Adjoining Hobart is another city, Glenorchy, with a population of 41,000, and together the two form what is called Greater Hobart.

Glenorchy was established soon after Hobart and was named by Governor Macquarie, who drew one of his many comparisons with Scotland — this time with a village on the Orchy River. The prefix "Glen" is derived from the Gaelic word "gleann", meaning tumbling waters.

Glenorchy was an important agricultural and horticultural area but, during the past 50 years it has become the base for many of the State's leading industries, some of which are open for inspection.

Industry at work

The famous Cadbury confectionery factory owned by Cadbury-Schweppes Pty Ltd is at Claremont. Tours are held regularly (except from the end of December to mid-January) and there's a chance to sample some of the "goodies" while watching the chocolate-making process. Children under eight are only allowed if carried by an adult, and details of visits can be obtained from Tasmanian Travel Centres.

The Electrolytic Zinc Co. at Risdon, one of the largest plants of this type, exports zinc and zinc alloys around the world. On weekdays, one to two hour inspections can be arranged with the Company.

Sheridan Domestic Textiles have a mill at Derwent Park, where a disposal centre sells seconds in dress, furnishing and bedding materials at bargain prices.

Restored cottage

In the early 1800s James Austin was transported to Australia for the theft of beehives worth 30/- and, on his release, he was granted 80 acres of land at what now is known as Austin's Ferry.

He built a cottage in 1809 and it has been restored by the Glenorchy City Council for community use. The cottage was originally named Baltonsborough Cottage, after Austin's birthplace. A signpost at Austin's Ferry on the main road indicates the way to the cottage.

Austin established the first trans-Derwent ferry service, which provided an important link for travel between Hobart and Launceston before the Bridgewater Causeway was built.

Glenorchy before 1900.

A hobby that grew — Alpenrail, in Claremont — is not only a large model railway, but also a scenic wonderland. Check Tasmanian Travel Centres for opening times.

There is an excellent recreation area and park at the Tolosa Street Reserve (shelter sheds and wood provided for barbecues) and the Poimena Reserve at Austin's Ferry is a 24 ha bushlands site with a variety of Australian native plants.

The modern Bowen Bridge links Glenorchy with Risdon Cove and the eastern shore of the Derwent.

Risdon Cove — history was made here

Risdon Cove is the only first settlement site of an Australian capital to survive in any semblance of its original form.

The two copper-topped pyramids are a design which evolved from simple geometric shapes of the Georgian style which influenced Tasmanian colonial architecture. They house historical items and plans of the site as well as details of the area's first settlers — the Aborigines.

A walk to the top of the hill, past ruins of the original store (the oldest stone structure in Tasmania), provides splendid views over the Cove. A flagpole stands on the site of the original flagstaff where roll call was held each day and people gathered to hear the latest colonial regulations. Marked areas show the position of the huts and the remains of Restdown, a property which was a home renowned for hospitality in the 19th century. Archaeological excavation began here in 1978 and the N.P.W.S., which controls the area, already has re-built some of the early structures, and the restoration programme aims to make the area a "living" rather than a static display.

Austins Cottage has pride of place at Austins Ferry.

Hut at Risdon Cove, site of the first European settlement.

The fort at Bellerive Bluff.

Bellerive — a ferry port for more than 100 years.

Many of Hobart's attractions are free.

Clarence — fort and beaches

Suburbs and towns on the eastern shore form part of the Clarence Municipality, the centre of which is in Bellerive, once a railhead for the Sorell and Cambridge lines.

A fort at Bellerive Bluff was built 100 years ago in response to fears of a Russian invasion. Now the area is preserved by the N.P.W.S.

Rokeby — old church

St Matthew's Church at Rokeby, 14 km from Hobart, has an organ which was originally brought from England and installed in St David's Cathedral. The graveyard contains the tomb of the Reverend Robert Knopwood, the first colonial chaplain of Van Diemen's Land.

Lots to see

From Rokeby the main road continues past the Tasmania Police Academy to Lauderdale and the beach front residential areas of Cremorne (bay and lagoon beaches), Clifton (good surf), Opossum Bay (sheltered beach) and South Arm (State Recreation Area, near an Army base and the Iron Pot Lighthouse — a focal point for seafarers, including yachtsmen in the annual Sydney to Hobart race).

On the return trip to Hobart a detour can be made at Lauderdale to Seven Mile Beach (an area true to its name with massive sand dunes at one end), where extensive picnic and recreation areas have been developed by the Lands Department. Acton Road can be followed to the Eastern Outlet from Hobart, and it's worth taking a further detour to Mt Rumney, from where there are superb panoramic views ...

Beaches, bushwalks, parks, old buildings ... many of Hobart's attractions are free. All that's necessary is a desire to join in the City's "unhurried good life".

Port Arthur — tranquillity replaces dread

South and South East

Hops, apples, historic sites and modern industries, all can be seen during trips in southern and south-eastern Tasmania.

Using Hobart as a base it's westward-ho for the fertile Derwent Valley with its postcard scenery and farmlands, south to fruit and timber areas of the D'Entrecasteaux, Huon and Esperance districts, and east to the classic town of Richmond and the beautiful Tasman Peninsula with its ruins of the infamous Port Arthur penal settlement.

Timber from the Huon and Channel areas has been used in many diverse projects; sleepers for the Trans-Siberian Railway, piers for the Melbourne docks. But it was fruit, especially apples, that really put Tasmania on the international map and led to it being labelled the "Apple Isle".

Exports of fruit have declined in the past decade, mainly because of competition from overseas countries, but orchards and associated activities still are a feature of the region, along with the timber and fishing industries.

When heading south from Hobart the most scenic route is the Channel Highway via Sandy Bay Road. Sandy Bay is noted for its beaches by the Derwent and another attraction on the main road is a Tudor Village.

A Touch of Tudor

Poliomyelitis victim John Palotta spent most of his life making a scale model of his English village in Kent. Buildings include a 14th century parish church, manor house and coaching inn — all made from dental plaster, matches, wire and paint. The church took two years to build, 2,000 matchsticks being finely split to hold stained glass windows.

An attraction for more than 30 years, the village is in Tudor Court, a restored stagecoach house.

A touch of Tudor in Sandy Bay.

Shot Tower, Taroona.

Shot Tower

Rising 66 m from a gully the Shot Tower is an imposing sight beside the Channel Highway just past the suburb of Taroona.

The Tower was built in 1870 by scotsman Joseph Moir using more than 8,000 individually curved and tapered sandstone blocks. When molten lead was dropped from the top of the Tower into water it would form perfect spheres of shot. Visitors with a head for heights can climb to a platform near the top.

At the base of the Tower there is a museum and tearooms with Tasmanian crafts on sale.

Kingston — Antarctic base

The beachside suburb of Kingston is favoured by swimmers and sailors of small yachts, and the Kingborough Sports Complex caters for a wide range of indoor activities. Horseriding is also popular. Kingston offers a full range of shops, including the Hythe Gallery with superb crafts.

At the junction of the Channel Highway and the Southern Outlet road is St Clement's Church, a quaint building made from Huon pine; on top of the spire is a weather cock which was installed to mark the occasion of the church becoming free of debt!

The Australian Antarctic Headquarters are 2km south of Kingston on the highway. It's open for inspection from 9 a.m. to 5 p.m. on weekdays, with display items including Mawson's sledge, a Polar pyramid tent typical of those used in the "Deep South" and photographs of work in the Antarctic. Hobart is used by vessels of many nations as their last port of call on the way to the southern continent.

19

The Channel Highway continues to North-West Bay, where there is a public golf course, and, if time is short, a return trip to Hobart can be made by way of Howden. Tinderbox (sheltered beach). Pierson's Point (lookout) and Blackman's Bay (beaches and a blowhole). The Sanctuary at Howden, an exotic Mediterranean-style mansion pool, library and gym, is a romantic spot for travellers to stop for Devonshire teas or leisurely lunches.

Margate — by the junction!

Passenger trains no longer operate on main lines in Tasmania, but at Margate Junction the last of the State's passenger trains, the Tasman Limited, has come to a final destination. Today the only "passengers" are the visitors who come to buy food and crafts in the carriages, which also house a fascinating model train world.

Eric Sablowski spent six months creating a replica of the southern German countryside and the 40 trains which puff and speed through villages and mountains are the same as those operating on the lines in Germany. Intricate details include models of a wedding party leaving the church, waterfalls and trees made from Tasmanian lichen. It is open from Tuesday to Sunday.

Geological feature

A huge moss-covered mound of stone on the roadside at Margate 19 km from Hobart once was thought to be a meteorite. In fact, it formed by river erosion of a layered sheet of debris hurled out of a volano about 20 million years ago. Margate has developed in the past few years as a favoured spot for "out of town" living and, as a result, basic shopping outlets have expanded. The town's prime importance is as a base for fishing fleets and small boat owners, and a fish processing plant is one of the main employers. There's the Dru Point Bicentennial Park, a bowls club and boating facilities, and just south of the town centre, roadside stalls offer a wide range of local produce.

A few kilometres away is the township of Electrona, which developed as a housing area for people working at the local carbide works. The works no longer operate, but the plant is used now for processing silica obtained from Tasmania's South-West.

Snug — re-built after fires

Snug was named by explorers who found this part of North West Bay provided a safe anchorage. However, Snug was anything but safe in 1967 when fire swept through southern Tasmania killing more than 60 people. Most of Snug's buildings were destroyed and a temporary village was established in caravans on the town's oval.

Today Snug belies the horror of those times, and this peaceful place is a popular caravan and camping spot, with a sheltered beach and boat launching facilities. Snug Tiers overlook the township and there's an easy walk to Snug Falls. A narrow road leads to the Tiers, with roadside parking at the walk entrance. It takes about 20 minutes to reach the falls and there are seats and shelters along the route.

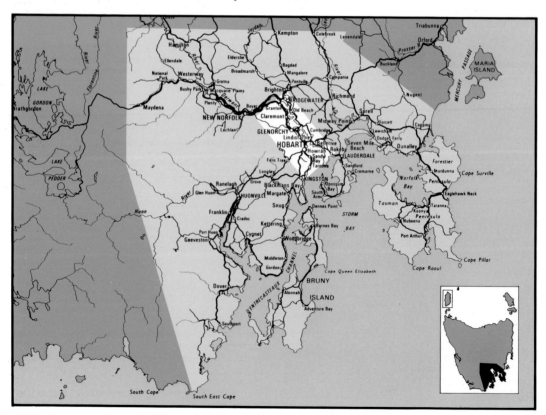

Beaches and museum

Continuing south on the highway a detour at Old Station Road leads to the beachside resort and State Recreation Area at Coningham and the Channel Historical and Folk Museum is one km past Snug. The Museum shows the history of the timber, whaling and scallop industries as well as a record of the 1967 fires. It is open daily, except Friday, from Boxing Day till the end of April but on Sundays only during the rest of the year.

Oyster Cove — Aborigine legacy

The last 40 full blood Tasmanian Aborigines spent their final days at Oyster Cove, a pretty inlet which, in earlier years, was frequented by the Aborigines because of the plentiful supply of shellfish. It was the wish of the last Aborigine, Trugannini, or Lalla Rookh as she sometimes was known, that her ashes would be scattered on seas near here — a request that finally was met 100 years after her death in 1876.

The Oyster Cove road winds round by the coast and re-joins the Channel Highway on the approach to Kettering, the mainland base of the Bruny Island ferry service.

Sailing on North-West Bay, near Coningham. The bay and nearby D'Entrecasteaux Channel are superb waters for boating.

Kettering — fishermen's shelter

Situated on a sheltered bay 34 km from Hobart, Kettering is a base for fishing boats and it also has a modern marina with facilities for up to 100 boats. The Huon pine-decked ferry "**Excella**" is dry-berthed by the marina, which was developed in conjunction with the Oyster Cove Inn, once the stately residence of a wealthy Queensland grazier. Seafoods are a speciality of the Inn, which offers comfortable accommodation in refurbished rooms in styles ranging from colonial to oriental.

A Smoke House and host farm also provide accommodation. Kettering has petrol and basic stores.

Two vehicular ferries operate services throughout the day to Bruny Island. Details of schedules for the 15-minute trip are available from Tasmanian Travel Centres. The D'Entrecasteaux Channel has some of the world's finest cruising waters, and craft available for hire from Kettering include self-sail Cavalier 26 yachts.

BRUNY ISLAND

In 1792 Admiral Bruni D'Entrecasteaux discovered that a channel separated the Tasmanian mainland and an island that was to become known as Bruny Island. The discovery was accidental — the result of a navigational error. North Bruny, with its open pasturelands, and South Bruny, which has more varied relief, are joined by a long, narrow isthmus.

Aborigines called this island Lunawannaalonna and the name lives on in the townships of Alonnah and Lunawanna. Trugannini, last of the full-blood Tasmanian Aborigines, belonged to a Bruny Island tribe.

The Island was sighted by Abel Tasman in 1642, and early visitors included Captain Tobias Furneaux (1773) and Captain James Cook. He landed at Adventure Bay in 1777 with William Bligh, who was then sailing master of H.M.S. Resolution. Bligh returned in 1788 and planted a number of fruit trees on the eastern side of the bay. Most were destroyed by fire, but one tree survived and is believed to be the first Tasmanian Granny Smith apple tree. A feature of South Bruny is the lighthouse; built in 1836 it is the second oldest in the Commonwealth.

Adventure Bay, Barnes Bay and Lunawanna are the main accommodation centres. There is a caravan park with on-site vans, a camping ground, holiday units, a country cottage, hostel, Karana Holiday Farm and Whalers' Inn Holiday Village.

Tasmania has prime surfing areas.

Museum of the Pacific

The Bligh Museum of Pacific Exploration at Adventure Bay was built from 26,000 handmade bricks brought from the old convict-built kiln at Variety Bay on North Bruny. It contains maps, documents, paintings and other items relating to history of the area, material about explorers of the South Pacific and Antarctic, and a collection of antique celestial and terrestrial globes. The Museum is open daily.

From whaling to surfing ...

Last century there was a whaling station on North Bruny and generations of timber workers have laboured on the heavily-timbered hillsides while fishermen have harvested the seas around the island.

Now it has special appeal also for holidaymakers and day trippers, including surfers who head for prime spots such as Cloudy Bay.

Prevailing conditions around Tasmania's coastline favour surfing, with good areas always available within a two-hour drive. No point in the State is more than 115 km from the sea. The most consistently good surfing areas are in the South and North-West. Popular destinations include Roaring Beach on the Tasman Peninsula and beaches near the mouth of the Mersey River at Devonport.

Timber cutters, Bruny Island.

Kettering is a boat haven and ferry base.

The D'Entrecasteaux Channel is never far from sight when travelling south on the Channel Highway from Kettering to Woodbridge, 43 km from Hobart.

Woodbridge — marine studies
Woodbridge is the site of a marine studies centre which gives schoolchildren a chance to observe and study the life of the waters that surround their island State.

Woodbridge has a hotel with restaurant and counter meals, shops and a hand-weaving studio 2 km off the highway. Along the foreshore there are many attractive picnic areas.

Fruit for sale
During December and January roadside stalls sell berries and other locally grown fruit. At Domeney's Cherry Farm 5 km south of Woodbridge, visitors can watch the fruit packing process and, as well as buying fruit for immediate enjoyment, can arrange to send it interstate or overseas.

At Middleton the Wolf family has produced berries for more than 100 years. Fresh strawberries, raspberries, black and red currants, gooseberries and blackberries are sold in season, while jams and frozen fruit are available at other times by arrangement.

Eric Wolf was born in Middleton in 1902 and has seen the changing fortunes of the timber and fruit industries in the area. His grandfather, a carpenter, came from Germany in the mid 19th century as one of the migrants recruited to work on projects such as construction of the Sorell Causeway. They were offered land grants and many headed for the East Coast, but Eric's grandfather decided to settle in the Channel district. He walked from Hobart in 1874 and selected land which was selling for two shillings an acre.

At the turn of the century the timber industry was thriving, and there were 50 pairs of sawyers working at Middleton. Eric recalls the great demand for shingles and palings, staves (for making casks), and logs for heavy construction work such as building wharves. Swamp gums, Stringy Bark and Tasmanian Oak were "worked" up Slab Road (which still retains this name) and hotels in the area did a roaring trade providing the meeting and eating places for timber workers. The hotels were also patronised by whalers from the Bruny Island station. Eric's family grew vegetables and one of his jobs as a boy was to take down supplies to the Middleton Hotel, which even had a lawn tennis court!

The hotel was destroyed in the 1967 bushfires, along with many other reminders of the past; the schoolhouse where Eric's wife, Hilda, taught more than 50 years ago was also burnt down.

Sailing ships and steamers would call at Middleton, Woodbridge, Kettering and Oyster Cove, and barges would anchor off-shore, waiting for lighters or flat irons to take out the timber. Jetty piles and bridge piles were hauled out of the bush with steel ropes and Eric remembered times when timber for railway sleepers was "as thick as a crop of oats" on the foreshore. There was plenty of excitement for Eric when, as a young boy, he went on his first day trip from the Channel to Hobart. Residents would wait eagerly for the arrival of boats such as the **Ivy**, **Rebecca** and **Nubeena** on which they would take their trip to "the big town".

The first berry fruits were planted at Oyster Cove, and it was from there that Eric's grandparents acquired their raspberry plants. This was the start of the family's commercial fruit business. Eric concentrated on apple orcharding; an industry which reached its peak in the 1960s. Varieties have changed a lot during the past 80 years, so names like Aromatic, Crows Egg, Rhode Island Green and Alexander are now just a memory. Many properties that Eric saw filled with orchards have become grazing areas but, inspite of the changes, the scenery in the Channel district continues to be superb.

Apple pickers at work early this century.

The Huon is renowned as an orcharding area.

Tranquil Huon River.

Skills of woodcrafts

The Channel Highway continues to the beach resort of Verona Sands (where there are fully equipped holiday units) and on to Gardner's Bay — from here a sign shows the way to "Talune Woodturning" which is run by craftsman Mike Jagoe.

Mike can be found on his 30 ha farm working with rainforest timbers such as Huon pine, sassafras, leatherwood, myrtle and blackwood. An audio visual presentation tells the story of Huon pine, Tasmania's unique timber, and also explains how Mike creates his products. There are gas barbecues and picnic areas and the farm is stocked with a variety of farm and native animals. Talune Woodturning is open daily.

There's a host farm at The Deepings, a base for more wood turning operations.

Cygnet — "French connection"

This fertile farming area west of the Huon River has had a variety of names. Originally called Port de Cygne (Swanport) by the French Admiral Bruni D'Entrecasteaux because of the many swans in the bay, it later became Port Cygnet and eventually just Cygnet. The town has hotels, a caravan park, youth hostel and farm accommodation. Paddle boats, dinghies with outboards and Canadian canoes are available for hire.

Produce of the land

Ciders made from the apples of the valley are among products sold at Lorraine Vineyards and Cygnet Brewery which open daily. Punnets of fresh strawberries, raspberries, logan-berries and blackberries are sold during the season, and frozen fruit packs are available during the rest of the year.

On the crest of a hill between Cygnet and Cradoc a sign post near some pines shows the way to Balfe's Hill Tea House. Up to 15 Jersey cows are milked daily to provide the milk, cream and cottage cheese used in the fare, which includes herb bread and, the specialties of the House, apple cake and cheesecake. Equally special are the jumpers, gloves and other woollen goods which are for sale. The Tea House also provides farm accommodation with twin rooms and shared facilities.

Huonville — commercial centre

Huonville is situated on the picturesque Huon River, named in 1792 after Captain Huon D'Kermandie, second in command to Admiral D'Entrecasteaux. Picnic areas line the river and, on weekends and public holidays, pedal boats and aqua bikes can be hired at the Esplanade.

A commercial centre, Huonville has a hotel, sporting and shopping facilities, including craft outlets. Atlantic salmon is a specialty at The Bistro, which also has cottage accommodation.

Emily and Charles Cowmeadow grew up in Franklin late last century. They married in 1910 and moved to Huonville, where there were only 20 houses! Not long before Charles had been among survivors of the steamship **Carpentaria** which sank on route from Franklin to Queenstown. When he finally made it to Queenstown he spent two years there splitting palings. In those years the Huon was a good source of labour for the Queenstown smelting and timber splitting industries. Many people also left the Huon district to seek their fortunes in New Zealand.

Charles saved his early wages of 18 pence for a nine-hour day until he could buy an orchard of his own. Apple boxes were made and packed by hand, and at one stage Charles was Australia's champion apple packer. For relaxation Charles would hunt wallaby and hare and go fishing. Highlights of the year for Huon families were the annual trip on the ferry **Excella** for a picnic at Bruny Island and the Shipwrights Point Regatta held on New Years Day. The latter was an occasion when people sometimes met for the first time since the previous regatta — something that is hard to imagine in these days of modern communication.

Superb scenery abounds in the Huon Valley.

Apple legacy

The Huon Valley Apple Industry Display, in an appleshed at Grove, on the northern outskirts of Huonville, features more than 400 varieties of apples, plus general information about the development of the industry.

Tasmanian apples were exported to England from the early 1880s. The fruit was packed into cases of split timber. Complaints from England about their bruised condition led to an investigation by Mr W.D. Peacock (a leading Tasmanian exporter of fruit). He devised a different type of case which enabled men to walk over them without bruising the fruit. This became known as the Peacock case and within a couple of years the long split timber cases were eliminated. In order to assess stacking requirements receiving clerks asked whether cases where "longies" or "dumpies". The "dump" became the standard fruit package until the 1920s when it was replaced with Canadian cases.

Early inventions

Apple industry exhibits at Grove include an 1843 peeler and corer (an American invention which could peel and core 25 apples every minute), examples of some of the apple case labels sent from Tasmania during the past century, and an apple grader developed by Joseph Lomas of Huonville in the late 1800s.

Vintage vehicles

The Tasman Antique Motor Museum is located at Ranelagh, a few kilometres north-west of Huonville. The Museum has restored and partly-restored vehicles, plus Australia's best collection of old enamel motor industry signs and old car parts! A rare 1927 Essex Boat-tail speedster is among items on display. The museum is open daily.

Another unusual exhibition in the area is at a craft centre which specialises in the production of carved appleheads. The centre is 9 km along a sideroad off the highway south of the bridge over the Huon River.

Franklin — rowing venue

Franklin, 8 km south of Huonville, is the oldest town in the Huon. The tranquil Huon River has provided an ideal setting for Australian rowing championships. Just past Franklin near Castle Forbes Bay, there is a craft and apple house. River and channel cruises operate from the Kermandie Hotel at Port Huon.

Geeveston — timber country

Geeveston, 31 km south of Huonville, was named after an English migrant William Geeves who settled here in 1850. It is now the administrative centre of the Esperance Municipality, the most southerly municipality in Australia, which extends to Macquarie Island 1,000 km south of Tasmania at the "entrance to the Antarctic"

Sawmills dot the area and there is a pulpmill 3 km from Geeveston. Woodchips for export to Japan have been produced here, but with uncertainty about the future of timber and associated industries residents are developing more tourism attractions. An old homestead, built in 1870, has been converted to a tourist and community centre. The town also has a hotel, shops and self-contained holiday cabins on a waterfront farm.

Geeveston is a base for forestry operations and the gateway to the Hartz Mountains National Park, 21 km away.

Apple packing about 1910.

Superb rainforests, rugged mountains

The Hartz Mountains National Park has many walking tracks, nature trails and picnic areas. The Arve Loop Road, one of Australia's most dramatic rainforest drives, runs north along the banks of the Arve River. At the Waratah Lookout, 24 km from Geeveston, there are picnic areas and a rock shelter. For the more adventurous, three-day rafting trips on the Picton and Huon Rivers are conducted during summer months (details from Tasmanian Travel Centres).

Snow-capped mountains in the winter, wildflowers, native trees and picturesque lakes make this a photographer's dream world. A track for bushwalkers leads to Mt Picton and the Arthur Range near Federation Peak. Rugged mountains give way to deep gorges, alpine mooreland and open heath.

Closer to Geeveston, the Tahune Forest Reserve (30 minutes drive from the town) is a delightful picnic spot, with covered barbecues, shelters and numerous walking tracks.

Dover — getting up steam

There aren't any white cliffs here, but there are links with Dover's namesake in England. Much of the timber exported from the Huon in the 19th century went to England and the Continent. As well as being used to pave the streets of London and, to build dykes in Holland, it was made into piles to support the famous pier at Dover, England. One of Australia's most southern towns, Dover is 43 km from Huonville, and the base for a fishing fleet and a fish processing industry. Fishing trips can be arranged with private boat captains.

Atlantic salmon farms developed recently near Dover have boosted both the local economy and employment opportunities.

Engines and apples

Years of labour and lots of love went into restoration of items at Casey's Living Steam Museum. A century-old Marshall engine was salvaged from the Raminea Mill, one of many which operated in this area in the late 19th and early 20th centuries. The Museum is housed in a former apple processing factory. It is the only fully steam-operated museum in Australia, and exhibits are powered by the original marine-type boiler. Opening times vary during the year. Check with Tasmanian Travel Centres. Dover has hotels (accommodation and counter meals), a caravan park, stores and petrol supplies (the last for motorists heading towards South East Cape).

Highway and by-ways

Southport is a small seaside resort and fishing and farming centre originally named Mussel Bay. The Huon Highway ends here, 27 km south of Dover, but secondary roads lead farther south. Rare endemic heath is found at the Southport Lagoon Wildlife Sanctuary, 10 km from Lune River.

A road branching off the highway, 21 km from Dover, leads to the Hastings Caves area, where there are three limestone caves, a thermal swimming pool where water all year round is about 27 degrees Celsius, a kiosk, barbecues, shelters and delightful picnic grounds with short bush walks.

Timber operations near Geeveston around 1900.

Cave tours

The caves were found in 1917 by timber workers from the Hastings Mill. The largest one, Newdegate Cave, was named after the Governor, Sir Francis Newdegate. Tours are conducted regularly throughout the day by N.P.W.S. officers and visitors are taken through lofty chambers, past stalactites, stalagmites, shawls and columns which have formed into strange and beautiful shapes.

The approach to Hastings is impossible to miss — a Natural Wood Art Centre (open daily) is "guarded" by Carved wooden giants!

Limestone formations at Hastings caves.

Lune River — ride the rails

Another section of the secondary road leads to Lune River, where philatelists are keen to have items postmarked from Australia's most southern post office. For a longer stay — perhaps while fossicking for gemstones — there are cabins (with a community kitchen) and a youth hostel.

The narrow-gauge railway track winding 6 km to the Deep Hole jetty and beach was originally used by limestone carriers.

The road continues on to Catamaran and Recherche Bay, where there's a 760 ha State Recreation Area.

To vary the return trip to Hobart (and see some spectacular views) it is worth heading north through Huonville, Grove and Longley and on to Fern Tree. From Longley a further alternative route travels via Sandfly, Kingston and the Southern Outlet road.

At Fern Tree, St Raphael's Church, with its leadlight windows, provides a "touch of Europe" amidst the mountain greenery, and a tavern provides comfort of another kind! A schoolroom, dwelling and church (complete with music) form focal points at Settlers Green Bush Village. The buildings were transported from their original locations and lovingly restored by a local family. The village is set amidst extensive mountain parklands that are ideal picnic sites. Cottage crafts and Devonshire teas are available.

From Fern Tree it's just 10 km to the heart of Hobart.

Fern Tree — a base for mountain walks and drives.

In the 1830s Richmond was the "Granary of Van Diemen's Land" — it has now risen to prominence as an historic village that should be included on every traveller's itinerary.

Richmond — a classic town

To reach Richmond, 24 km from Hobart, take turnoffs from the Eastern Outlet just past Tunnel Hill and at Cambridge, a base for light industry, helicopter and light aircraft operations.

Richmond, a classified historic town without equal in Australia, is the site of one of the earliest penal institutions in the island.

Members of Lieutenant Bowen's party, moving east from Risdon Cove, found coal here by the river, and Richmond on the Coal River soon developed as an important granary, with mills driven by wind, water and steam. The village was also a crossing place for travellers going to Sorell and the East Coast. The stone bridge was built in 1823 and it is the oldest bridge still standing in Australia.

When the Sorell Causeway was built in 1872, Richmond was by-passed by traffic from Hobart to Port Arthur, and part of the town's charm derives from its lack of hustle and bustle. The town has a number of delightful eating places. Prospect House, a Georgian style mansion, offers food and accommodation, while Ma Foosies and Ashmore House specialise in Devonshire teas and light lunches. At the Richmond Maze and Tea Rooms there are both refreshments and frustrations!

The variety of accommodation also includes a caravan park with on-site vans, barbecue, tennis and games facilities, a host farm, holiday cabins catering for up to 30 guests, and self-contained colonial cottages classified by the National Trust and dating back to the 1830s.

Richmond Bridge is more than 160 years old.

Bridge Street, Richmond

Churches and galleries

Other places of interest are the Gothic Revival style St John's Church, the oldest Roman Catholic church in Australia; the Georgian styled St Luke's Church of England, which features a clock originally used in the tower of St David's Cathedral in Hobart; Saddler's Court Gallery (formerly a saddlery), with its excellent display of paintings, pottery, cards and other gift items; the Peppercorn Gallery, specialising in wooden, silver, pewter and glass creations; the Richmond Granary and Richmond Galleries. An exclusive fibre boutique, Mostly Mohair, has the latest handcrafted fashion knitwear, most of which is made from Tasmanian-produced raw materials. Visitors of all ages are tempted at Sweets and Treats, with its old-fashioned lollies and up-to-the-minute ice-creams. A courtyard bakery and specialist Australiana shops satisfy every temptation! The aroma of potpourri, lavender and other fragrances fill Molly Greenes, a tiny shop that has gifts for tiny people as well as older ones who like pretty things. Other collectables are found in the Miller's Cottage, which contrasts with the grander restored colonial buildings.

Time changes all things, but Richmond seems destined to remain a town of living history.

Oldest of gaols

Richmond has the best-preserved convict gaol in Australia and the oldest part pre-dates Port Arthur by five years. Built in 1825, it was used as a gaol and to house convicts working in road gangs. It is open daily and now houses relics of the past, including diaries, records, clothing and tools of its former inmates and their overseers.

A gaol with many tales to tell.

St Lukes Church of England.

St Johns — the oldest Roman Catholic Church in Australia.

Return another way

To return to Hobart by a longer route, turn off at Richmond and follow the road to Campania and Colebrook. Colebrook, 54 km from Hobart, was originally called Jerusalem, but, as it was the site of a convict probation station, authorities thought the name was inappropriate. After a further 19 km the road joins the Midland Highway near Jericho (see page 92).

Another alternative route starts just south of Campania and travels through the farming district of Tea Tree and on to Bridgewater, 19 km north of Hobart. The causeway linking Bridgewater and Granton on the western shore of the Derwent River was built in the 1830s by convicts undergoing secondary punishment in chain gangs. The causeway was guarded from a watch house at Granton.

Confined quarters

The watch house was built in 1838 and today provides a display of relics from the early days, including a solitary cell 50 cm square and 2 m high — the smallest used in Australia. Granton also has two other establishments with a claim to fame. The Hilltop Restaurant was the first licensed restaurant in Tasmania and is near one of the State's oldest hostelries, the York Hotel.

From Hobart the Northern Outlet road leads to Granton and the start of the Lyell Highway, the main route to Queenstown.

The Derwent River traverses much of Tasmania as it wends its way from near Lake St Clair to Hobart, but few areas could compare with the beauty of the district known as the Derwent Valley, which extends from New Norfolk to Ouse.

Boyer — mills changed the area

The Australian Newsprint Mills on the eastern side of the Derwent River produce 60% of Australia's newsprint. The complex is open for inspection at 2 pm on Tuesday, by arrangement. It is one of only two newsprint mills in Australia, and when it was established more than 40 years ago the area changed from a rural to an industrial one. Many farm labourers sought jobs at the mill and it still is the district's main source of employment. For activity of another kind, there are regular meetings on the opposite shore at the Bridgewater Speedway.

New Norfolk — picturesque

This historic town, 38 km from Hobart, was originally called Elizabeth Town, but was renamed by settlers who moved there in 1808 from Norfolk Island. The Island had been abandoned because of its isolation.

The New Norfolk area is renowned for its hops; experimental production had started as early as 1822 in Hobart. There have been many changes since then, however, and most hops grown today are seedless varieties. An increasing number are pelletised before being shipped to breweries around the world.

Hops — then and now

Hop farming methods of the 19th century can be studied at the Oast House Museum which is situated in hop kilns which operated for more

Hop kilns dot the Derwent Valley.

than 100 years. The work of Tasmanian artists and craftsmen is on display in an adjacent art gallery, and pottery is made on the site. These attractions are in Tynwald Park, formerly the grounds of a colonial miller's house which now offers accommodation and meals.

Churches and inns

New Norfolk has many other historic features. Tasmania's oldest existing church, St Matthew's Church of England, has a visitors' and craft centre in the adjoining St Matthew's Close. One of the most famous guests at the Bush Inn (established in 1825) was Dame Nellie Melba, and an autographed photo of the famous singer is among treasured possessions of Joe Cowburn, whose family owned the inn for more than 50 years.

The Cowburn family also had interests in the New Norfolk and Star and Garter Hotels in the 1890s, and other brewing and hotel establishments such as the Jolly Hatter's Brewery (now the Black Prince Hotel in Hobart), the Traveller's Rest in Sandy Bay, the Elwick Hotel at Glenorchy, and inns at Carrick, Evandale and Zeehan.

Joe was born in 1905 and his early recollections included those of the "hop holidays" when schools of the district closed during the hop picking season so children could work and so boost the family income. Special trains would bring hop pickers from Hobart to Bushy Park. In total about 5,000 people were employed picking hops in the fields.

The Bush Inn, New Norfolk, a meeting place for many years.

A peg factory (now one of the State's largest antique stores) was an important employer; more than 120 people worked on production of one million pegs each week. The factory was famous for its sassafras "dolly pegs".

The Bush Inn was a genuine community meeting place — even the Methodists held their first meeting in the pub! It was here, too, that discussions were held about the need for a bridge across the river. Over the years there have been four bridges; one of those who worked on their construction was the father of Lord Casey, a former Australian Governor-General.

The Bush Inn still is among the New Norfolk establishments offering "lodgings and fine fare", but these days you don't have to pay a shilling extra for a fire in your room. The Old Colony Inn, once a hostelry for soldiers, is now a landmark for travellers, many of whom sample the famous Devonshire teas and trout luncheons.

Youth hostel with a difference

As well as caravan and camping accommodation, New Norfolk has a quaint youth hostel in an octagonal timber building which was once the tollhouse for travellers crossing the bridge.

The town also has facilities for swimming (in a heated, Olympic pool), tennis, bowls and golf. For a truly thrilling trip, Australia's only "white water" jet boat covers a 19 km circuit between New Norfolk and Plenty, on the hour between 10 am and 4 pm, daily. Trips can be combined with four-wheel drive explorations.

The Lyell Highway continues over the bridge to Hayes, Gretna, Hamilton and Ouse

New Norfolk's youth hostel once was a toll house.

(then on to the West Coast), while a minor road travels up the western shore of the river to Plenty, Bushy Park, Westerway, National Park and Maydena.

Hayes — prison farm

This is the base for the State's Prison Farm. Travellers can sample earth's bounty at roadside stalls run by the other locals.

Gretna — interesting cemetery

The Gretna Green Hotel, 55 km from Hobart, has accommodation and counter meals — but no marriage celebrant! Holiday cabins are available for hire at Gretna, where there is an interesting church, St Mary's, and an old cemetery.

Hamilton — colonial accommodation

Situated on the Clyde River, this classified historic town, 70km from Hobart, has a number of interesting buildings, including the council chambers, cottages and the Glen Clyde Craft Centre. Accommodation is available in Emma's, George and Victoria's colonial sandstone cottages, on a rural property, in the old School House and the Hamilton Inn. At the Hamilton Sheep Centre, groups can view shearing and other activities associated with sheep farming.

Ouse — rich farmlands

Ouse is the centre of a lush agricultural district and the starting point for a round trip to hydro electric schemes at Wayatinah, Liapootah, Tarraleah and Tungatinah and on to Bronte Lagoon. Ouse, 70 km from Hobart, has a hospital, food stores and hotel accommodation. The West Coast "capital", Queenstown, is a further 86 km away at the end of the Lyell Highway (see page 78).

Journeying up the western bank of the Derwent from New Norfolk a stop should be made at Plenty to see the Salmon Ponds.

A fishy story

Spacious parklands at the Salmon Ponds form delightful picnic and rest areas all year round. The first brown and rainbow trout in the southern hemisphere were raised here in 1864, making possible the stocking of lakes and streams in Australia and New Zealand. Details of the development are outlined in a museum. Trout is a specialty at the restaurant!

Bushy Park — hop centre

Autumn trees are a glorious sight in the Styx River Valley at Bushy Park. This was once the biggest hop growing area in the southern hemisphere, but most of the smaller holdings now have been phased out.

A brick kiln, erected by hop pioneer Ebenezer Shoobridge in 1867, has some unusual tablets, including one which could be prophetic, "Union is Strength" — it is in the fields, along the timber kilns.

Westerway — crafts and holiday farm

At Westerway, wooden craft goods are available for sale. Accommodation in the area includes the Hillcrest Holiday Farm, complete with Old Macdonald and all his animals, at Ellendale, and cosy, century-old Hopfield Cottages.

National Park — trout and falls

The gateway to the Mt Field National Park is 73 km from Hobart. Attractions at the National Park township include the Russell Falls Trout Farm, one of the most technically advanced in Australia. Visitors can feed the fish, ducks, peacocks and other wildlife. Fresh fish are available for sale. There are tearooms, a kiosk, and extensive picnic grounds with barbecues. Accommodation is available in an hotel, self-contained units, huts and a caravan park.

Russell Falls, discovered in 1856, are just a 10 minute walk and well worth the effort — the 40 m falls are a magnificent sight. There are numerous falls and bush walks in the Mt Field National Park, and Lake Dobson (15 km from National Park township) is at the base of the Mt Mawson ski-fields.

Maydena — timber country

Maydena, 85 km from Hobart, is a base for forestry operations, huge log trucks now travelling the roads along which bullocks used to haul their loads. There is a youth hostel at Maydena and this is the starting point for the Gordon Road to Strathgordon in the South West. On the return trip there is an alternative route to Hobart turning off the Lyell Highway 2 km south of New Norfolk. The road winds over hills to Molesworth and Collinsvale and joins the Hobart Northern Outlet at Berriedale. From here there is a view across to the Moorilla Estate, one of Tasmania's leading commercial vineyards. Producers began experimenting with grapes in the late 1950s and the State now is gaining widespread recognition for its red and white table wines, the prime aim being to produce wines of quality, rather than quantity.

Old school house at Hamilton.

Fertile farmlands of the Derwent Valley.

Tasmania has some challenging ski slopes and, while some facilities are basic, there are plans for further grooming of slopes and development of accommodation and access. The two main areas — Mt Mawson (1,310 m) in the Mt Field National Park, 75 km west of Hobart, and Ben Lomond, 64 km south east of Launceston — are much closer to main population centres than ski resorts in other States and are also much cheaper.

Mt Mawson has three rope tows and a beginner's tow, with numerous slopes for accomplished skiers. Boots, skis and stocks can be hired and there's a kiosk. No public accommodation is available on the slopes but there are N.P.W.S. huts at Lake Dobson and at the township of National Park, where there is also a caravan park. It is hoped that a chairlift eventually will take visitors from the car park at Lake Dobson to the slopes, but at the moment the journey involves a half-hour walk up a steep half-kilometre stretch.

Chains are necessary for vehicles at both Mt Mawson and at Ben Lomond during the winter.

In the North
The northern slopes are reached via Blessington, but the final section of the road up Jacobs Ladder is very steep and narrow. Buses and four-wheel drive vehicles can be hired in Launceston or from the base of the mountain. There's a kiosk, tavern bar (hot meals throughout the day) and a family day shelter. Limited tavern accommodation is available, but huts are owned privately or by clubs. Facilities include six Poma lifts and two T-bars. Ski gear can be hired, and skiing instruction is available.

The 16,000 ha Ben Lomond National Park is a magnificent area for walking, climbing and photography.

Cross country skiing also is gaining popularity. The western field at Cradle Mountain and Mt Rufus in the Cradle Mountain Lake St Clair National Park are particularly good for this sport.

The first parties to test their prowess at skiing in Tasmania gathered at Mt Field National Park and on Mt Wellington in 1922. The State's first ski club was formed three years later — the major clubs today are the Southern Tasmania Ski Association and the Northern Tasmanian Alpine club. The average season for skiing lasts for about 12 weeks.

Winter skiing.

For nearly half a century the history of Tasman Peninsula was intricately entwined with that of the convicts sent to serve their sentences in what was intended to be a reformatory penal establishment at Port Arthur. Those who did not "toe the line" would often be sent to labour in harsh conditions at coal mines and quarries in other parts of the peninsula.

For decades, details about the penal settlement were glossed over, but now promoters are proud to call this "Convict Country".

The Tasman Highway travels eastwards from Hobart and past the airport, which is near Seven Mile Beach, a recreation area that includes The Pines Resort with villas, a licensed restaurant, tennis, windsurfing and other sporting facilities. Midway Point and Sorell are the next highway towns.

Named after Governor Sorell, this is one of the State's oldest towns. In 1824 the town was captured by bushranger Matthew Brady's gang, who imprisoned the soldiers of the garrison and most of the citizens. It was one of his last exploits; he died on the gallows in 1826.

Sorell has general stores and a caravan park and is at the junction of the Tasman and Arthur Highways, with Port Arthur 73 km away.

About 6 km out of Sorell a secondary road leads to the beach-side areas of Lewisham, Dodges Ferry and Carlton (noted for its surf), later re-joining the highway.

Tasmanian timbers are a feature of the Lilac Gallery, set on a farm by the highway at Copping, where there is a fine selection of artworks, pottery and other craft items.

Unusual payment at the Denison Canal, Dunalley.

Unusual payment

Motorists held up at Dunalley while boats pass through the Denison Canal have a chance to watch an unusual method of payment. The toll for boat owners is $2 and a can of beer!

That was something Abel Tasman didn't have to do when he landed near here in 1642, an event which is commemorated in a memorial on the Dunalley foreshore.

The town is a base for a fish processing industry, and has a crayfish restaurant, take-away food stores, fish tackle supplies and a hotel established in 1866, where counter lunches are available. Keen gardeners often can be seen gathering seaweed on beaches between Dunalley and Murdunna (store with "snacks" and tourist information).

Eaglehawk Neck — memorable

Spectacular views over Pirates Bay (named when convicts captured the schooner **Seaflower** here) and Eaglehawk Neck, a narrow strip of land which separates Forestier and Tasman Peninsulas, delight photographers. Near the Neck is the Tessellated Pavement, where a rock shelf has been split into tiles by earth movement and rock erosion. Eaglehawk Neck offers accommodation and meals in a refurbished hotel and a motel, both good bases for people heading out to sea in search of bluefin tuna. Fully-equipped boats are available for hire, and Australian record tuna catches have been set here. Other fish which lure fishermen to this part of the State between January and June include marlin, stripy tuna and Spanish mackerel.

Barriers of all kinds

Unusual geological formations in the area include a blowhole, which has claimed a number of lives, the Devil's Kitchen and Tasman's

Tesselated pavement at Eaglehawk Neck.

Arch, reached by way of Doo Town, where residents have named their properties by such quaint names as "I Doo" and "This'll Doo me".

The isthmus is the only land access to the Tasman Peninsula and convicts from Port Arthur were deterred from escape by stories of sharks in the bay (never proven) and a cordon of soldiers and savage guard dogs which patrolled the Neck. Usually those who did try were soon recaptured, but one who was successful was the bushranger Martin Cash; he escaped by swimming hidden by a floating branch.

The Neck has not only proved a barrier to man but also to a creature of another kind —the octopus. Several years ago an octopus breeding industry was established in the bay when large numbers were found following what appeared to be an old migratory route, probably established when a channel led out to sea, before the Neck developed.

Taranna — new attractions

Many towns on the peninsula which previously were of little interest to the visitor, have become stopping points because of recently developed attractions. Taranna (an Aboriginal word meaning hunting ground) is one of them.

Australia's first railway ran between Port Arthur and Taranna, and it was manned, literally, by four convicts who were harnessed to a carriage laden with passengers and supplies. A replica of the railway is on display in the grounds of Norfolk Galleries, once the Norfolk Bay Convict Station.

Devils and apples

Attitudes are changing now, but in the past the only things many people associated with Tasmania were its apples and Tasmanian devils (an image created largely by the influence of American cartoons). Both these traditional features abound at the Tasmanian Wildlife and Nature Park situated in a former Taranna orchard.

The devils are marsupials and resemble a small, sturdy dog. A pest to hunters, they hide in burrows during the day and come out to hunt at night. They can kill small animals but gather much of their food by scavenging; they clean out a carcass so effectively that it is sometimes possible to simply lift the fleece of a sheep which, along with a tiny section of jawbone, may be all that remains.

The number of Tasmanian devils is increasing, but the Tasmanian tiger appears to be extinct. Visitors to the Park can view a rare film of a tiger in the Hobart Zoo in the 1930s, and learn something about this species which "plagued" 19th and early 20th century farmers.

Tasmanian devils. Their numbers are increasing.

The Park is open daily and there are barbecue, picnic and toilet facilities.

A few hundred metres past the Park there is a road to the western side of the peninsula and the towns of Koonya, Premaydena, Nubeena and Saltwater River ...

Lionel Locke's father arrived on the Tasman Peninsula five years after the last convicts left, but one of Lionel's most vivid recollections concerned the ardent crusade of his parents to abolish anything "convict". It was not until later that Lionel realised they were "protecting" him from the knowledge that many of the local families were related to convicts.

Schooling was compulsory for children between 7 and 13 years of age if they lived within 5 miles of the school. But Lionel also spent a fair share of his time with his father, an early blacksmith and wheelwright on the peninsula. His father decided to become an orchardist and bought Pomona, a property at Impression Bay.

Young Lionel found it an ideal site for another reason — he could observe the Royal Navy manoeuvres; a squadron would spend several months in Norfolk Bay each year after the Hobart Regatta. The flagship would anchor in front of Pomona and the Navy's presence provided a number of bonuses for the locals. Lionel's father gained a Navy contract to supply mutton for 2/3d per dressed carcase, and, on fine evenings, the ship bands gave concerts for the local community.

Lionel had to help his father in the orchard and on the second of the family properties, Valley Farm, which had been established originally to supply food to the various convict establishments on the peninsula.

The Lockes experimented with pear production and at the 1910 Koonya Show they presented 65 varieties. In partnership with another local farmer, Dr Benjafield, Lionel's father went on to become Tasmania's biggest pear grower. The system of using trays to hold pears during shipment to England was conceived here, and when the Lockes received two guineas for a tray of pears delivered at the time of the coronation of George V it was the talk of the district for years.

Life has its lighter moments — like the time when Mick Paul got a new set of dentures. He put them on top of a fence post while he did some ploughing. After a couple of rounds he stopped the bullocks and decided to give his new teeth a trial. As he walked towards the dentures, down swooped a magpie and flew off with them!

Lionel's mother was the first postmistress on the peninsula to have a phone; it was introduced so the Navy could "keep in touch with headquarters" during manoeuvres. Their presence was felt in other quarters too. During gunnery practice residents had to keep their windows open so they were not broken by concussion of the 8" guns. However, even these precautions were to no avail, when in 1911 H.M.A.S. Australia fired her 12" guns. Many open windows were shattered. It was the last year of the annual exercises!

The Koonya saleyards opened in the late 1880s and were on a par with those at Sorell and Huonville. At this time butter and cheese production was also important, farmers receiving the princely sum of 3d or 4d for a pound of butter. By the same token, they only had to pay about 2/- for a pair of boots and 1/- for working trousers.

Lionel remembered prices well because his father also ran a store until 1908. Nowadays the same sort of items he sold and used are displayed in a Country Life Museum at Koonya. Here there is also a pioneer schoolhouse. The museum is open at weekends and on public holidays.

Cascades cottage at Koonya.

Colonial accommodation

A restored convict building on a former outstation of Port Arthur now provides colonial accommoation at Cascades, Koonya. Prisoners worked the nearby Cascade Quarry. Guests stay in what formerly served as a hospital. The outstation was once a village for about 400 convicts, administrators, guards and private citizens.

This is one of a series of establishments providing "colonial holidays" in Tasmania.

For a "real life" trip, a half-size train winds through the bushland beside the aqua waters of the bay between the mill and the Fox and Hounds.

Tudor in Tasmania

The Fox and Hounds Hotel provides a touch of Olde England with its Tudor style and fire side comforts. It has self-contained accommodation and a licensed restaurant (the original beer pulls from the Victorian era are a special feature in the bar).

Coal mines at Saltwater River — a notorious outpost.

Shingle-splitting ... an old art lives on.

Horseriding is another attraction at Koonya, with facilities at the Seaview Ranch.

Saltwater River — coal mines

Saltwater River is reached via Premaydena, site of a leading Australian quail farm. Despite the beautiful aqua sea and lush grass surroundings, there is an unearthly stillness about the ruins of the coal mining establishment at Saltwater River. It was the place most dreaded by convicts. The mines were a centre for harsh secondary punishment for convicts who fell foul of the authorities.

Even the fire which led to abandonment of the mine in 1877 could not wipe out traces of their misery. Part of the complex is open for inspection and shows 18 cells in a row, nine opening on to one corridor and nine on to another. These alternating cells prevented prisoners from having even minimal contact.

Nubeena — sandy beaches

Nubeena (the Aboriginal word meaning crayfish) is the largest town on the peninsula and is a good base for visitors who want to spend time exploring long, sandy beaches and dunes such as those at Roaring Beach and White Beach. Nubeena has a camping ground, self-contained units, and the Fairway Lodge Country Club complex, which has self-contained and motel-type units, half tennis courts, a nine-hole golf course and heated indoor pool. A licensed restaurant is just a short walk away.

A road leads from Nubeena to Port Arthur 11 km to the East, or you can return to the Arthur Highway and stop en-route at other attractions.

Timber for centuries

The Bush Mill stands on a site of one of the peninsula's 19th century milling settlements.

As steam builds up from the sawmill a shingle-splitter goes about his work (many of the products from locally cut swamp gum being used in restoration work at Port Arthur), a blacksmith turns out horseshoes and fire-side sets, and a woodturner crafts items from Tasmanian timbers. One can travel back in time to the days of the timber-cutters' camps, sawpits and wooden tramways and, at the end of the "trip", there are delightful Devonshire teas, light lunches or a cray feast (to be organised in advance for party or group bookings).

Stay a while

A variety of accommodation has been developed at Port Arthur in recent years. There is a motel, youth hostel, host farm with amenities for five people, a guest house, and the New Plymouth Holiday Village, which is ideal for families. It has log cabins, play areas and a licensed restaurant. The Garden Point Caravan Park is set in extensive grounds and has self-contained sites. Canoes and dinghies can be hired near the award-winning caravan park.

Port Arthur — "feel" history

The most famous of Tasmania's penal establishments, Port Arthur, still carries the "scars" from the years 1830 to 1877 when thousands of convicts were based in what the area's namesake, Governor George Arthur, described as a "natural penitentiary".

About half of the 74,000 convicts transported to the island were sentenced to seven-year terms, while one in five were "lifers". More than half had previous convictions, although offences often were slight by today's standards. About 14,000 female convicts were transported but women were not sent to Tasman's Peninsula.

Of all the convicts landed on these shores approximately only one in 20 was sentenced to a penal settlement and they were the ones who had committed serious offences or a series of minor ones.

Excavation reveals secrets
The original convicts were housed in wooden huts and the site of these structures is among those being excavated under Commonwealth and State restoration and conservation projects.

The area now is maintained by the N.P.W.S. which has converted the old asylum into a visitor reception centre, museum with records of transportees and other reminders of the not so glorious past, and an audio visual theatre.

The model prison, with its solitary punishment cells, still sends shivers down the spines of people who step into its confines. Prisoners sometimes had to stay in small cells for weeks, a gaoler being their only visitor. They endured a "silent system" of punishment.

A number of buildings are being restored, and the 1848 junior medical officer's house often is used as a display centre. A house formerly occupied by the Roman Catholic chaplain is among other buildings that have regained their former "status".

Ruins of the Port Arthur church.

Church of spires
The church, with its 13 spires representing Christ and his apostles, provides a focal point at Port Arthur, and is one of the most readily recognised sights in Australia. It was never consecrated because it was used by several denominations, and, like most other buildings, it later was a victim of fires which swept through the area; this destruction of the monuments of the penal system was considered fortuitous by many people ... However, as far back as the turn of the century visitors were flocking to Port Arthur, and today's attractions are mainly based on past activities.

Interest all around
One-hour mini-bus tours which leave the historic site six times daily (except Thursday), give an insight into many aspects of the early life in the area.

There are descriptions of the Point Puer Boys Prison, established 5 km from the main settlement so that 10-18 year old prisoners could be separated from adult convicts. It operated from 1834 to 1848. For a less "depressing" experience the tour also includes a visit to the Remarkable Cave, a massive coastal arch formation. By contrast, spectacular coastal views are obtained from a seaplane that is operated during the Summer by Wilderness Air, and it's also possible to travel around the ruins in a horse-drawn coach. Audio tours can be hired at the information office in the car park. Armed with a tape player and a map, visitors are guided round the settlement by the dramatised voice of 1840s convict, Frank MacNamara. Tours of another kind — day trips in four-wheel drive vehicles — concentrate on natural attractions such as rainforests and secluded beaches.

The original film version of Marcus Clarke's story "For the Term of His Natural Life" is shown each evening at the Broad Arrow. Much of the film for this silent movie classic was shot on location in the Port Arthur area in 1926.

Large burial grounds
The Isle of the Dead, in the middle of the bay, was the burial ground for 1,769 convicts and 180 soldiers, prison officials, police and settlers. Convicts were buried in communal graves, while elaborate headstones carved by convicts marked the graves of others. Today, visitors stepping ashore from cruises on the **Bundeena** (regularly throughout the day except from mid-June to early August), find only peace and tranquility.

An extensive cemetery also existed at Jetty Point (originally Eaton's Point) on Impression Bay. In the early 1840s a convalescent geriatric centre was established at Impression Bay. Convicts sent there were chronically ill and disabled, and most of them finally were buried in the cemetery. It was a burial ground also for convicts from the Cascades and the coal mines. At least 1,000 people have been laid to rest here.

Across the northern tip of the point two acres were set aside for burial of free settlers, and that area became a tourist attraction at the turn of the century when steamers used to bring visitors from Hobart. (Recognising the potential, authorities arranged to clear the "free area", but the convict graves were left covered with growth!).

Panorama of past and present
Looking down on Port Arthur from Palmer's Lookout it is hard to believe so much has changed in just 150 years or so. Tourists now hire horses from the Semaphore Farm, once a vital link in the semaphore telegraph system which helped authorities communicate with Hobart in a matter of minutes; people picnic on the foreshore on which the convicts assembled to be transferred to Hobart when Port Arthur was abandoned as a penal settlement in 1877.

Transportation had been abolished in 1853. The area then had an uncertain future ... now its future is assured — all because of the past.

East Coast

Isolation, poor communications and bush-rangers all contributed to the difficulties of the pioneers on the East Coast (which extends from Eddystone Point to Maria Island) and for many life became a day to day battle for survival. A number of the convicts who served their time at the Rocky Hills and Waterloo Point establishments were among those who chose to stay in the area and help lay the foundations for the wool, grain, beef and fishing industries which are still important today.

The pioneers lived from the bush; local stone and timbers were used to build dwellings, while hunting provided income as well as food. Riches still are being reaped from the harvesting of logs for the building industry and woodchip exports.

Coastal transport was vital in the 19th century, but now the main links are by road and many of the old jetties have disappeared. The Tasman Highway runs between Hobart and Launceston via Orford and St Helens, the Lake Leake Road connects Campbell Town in the Midlands with Swansea on the East Coast, and an inland road from Conara to St Marys follows the course of the South Esk River.

Noted for its moderate climate, the East Coast is a popular holiday area for Tasmanians who are lured by long sandy beaches, good fishing waters, bushland and numerous man-made attractions.

Coles Bay is noted for its beaches.

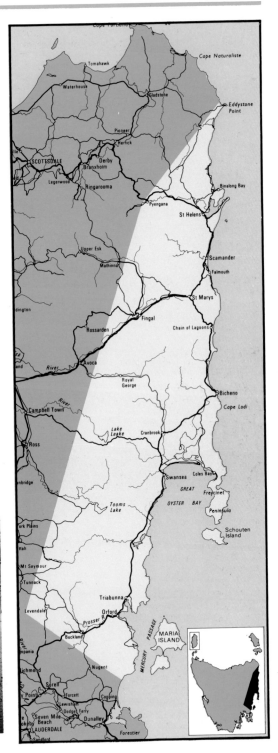

The Tasman Highway heads north at Sorell (26 km from Hobart) and then winds eastwards to Buckland, where the regular congregation at the Church of St John the Baptist is boosted by hundreds of visitors who call to see the famous stained glass east window, said to have been installed originally in a church built centuries before at the site of the Battle of Hastings. Later the Battle Abbey was badly damaged and it was never restored, but one of its windows was given to the Reverend Fox by the Marquis of Salisbury. It was installed in the Buckland Church in 1849, Mr Fox being the first rector.

Refreshments and counter lunches offered to travellers at Ye Olde Buckland Inn are just as welcome today as they were a century ago when coach drivers stopped here to prepare for the 18 km haul to Orford. Remains of the old coach road can be seen across the river when approaching Orford from the South.

Orford — boats big and small

Orford is a holiday resort and base for hire boats — canoes, dinghies and paddle boats on the Prosser River (named after an escaped prisoner who was recaptured on its banks) and a boat from Orford can be chartered for fishing and cruising.

Orford has bayside camping and caravan park, flats, motel (licensed) and colonial accommodation at Holkham House, where even house-trained pets are welcome! For relaxation, there are beaches, a golf course, bowling rink and horseriding.

Louisville — kelp, alginates and now tourists

It is hard to imagine this resort complex once was the base for a kelp harvesting and alginates industry. Situated between Orford and Triabunna on Prosser Bay, it has self-contained units, a 300-seat convention centre, a restaurant, tavern, indoor and outdoor pools, squash courts, sheltered boat moorings and a marina. The Eastcoaster resort is serviced by the **Maria Lady**, a ferry which runs regular services across the Mercury Passage to Maria Island. A charter boat also operates from Triabunna and the island has a landing strip for light aircraft.

Orford, a popular holiday resort.

MARIA ISLAND

The peace of Maria Island belies its convict past. Emus, Cape Barren geese, wallabies and Forester kangaroos roam freely amid ruins, restored buildings and around the hills.

Maria was chosen in 1825 as the site for Tasmania's second penal settlement (the first was at Macquarie Harbour on the West Coast). The settlement was abandoned in 1832, but 10 years later convicts were again sent to the Darlington establishment in the north of Maria Island. In subsequent years the island's chequered career was associated with the silk, wine and cement industries.

Now the island is a national park and wildlife sanctuary. Many of its old buildings have been restored by the N.P.W.S. including the penitentiary (where rooms are used now as "bunkhouses" by visitors), the old coffee palace, and messroom. There are extensive camping grounds, but no provisions or equipment are available.

The Island is a paradise for bushwalkers, swimmers, skin divers and fishermen. One of the short walks is from Darlington to the limestone Fossil Cliffs. Another leads to the southern end of Hopground Beach to the fascinating patterns of the sandstone cliffs.

Isolation, once a barrier to development on Maria Island, has proved beneficial in the long term — it has helped preserve this unique segment of our historical and natural heritage.

Sandstone formations on Maria Island.

The old settlement at Darlington, Maria Island.

Maria Island from Orford.

Triabunna — haven from the sea

Charter and fishing boats use this sheltered inlet, 8 km north of Orford, as a base, while farther round the bay, the tall timbers of the East Coast forests are processed at a woodchip plant. Triabunna was a whaling station and garrison town when Maria Island was a penal settlement. Fishing trips can be arranged here, catches including striped marlin and tuna which follow south-bound ocean currents. The town has a visitor information centre, hotel, motel (with pool), caravan and camping accommodation, restaurants and stores.

Many buildings of early settlers on the East Coast were made from Oyster Bay Pine, and now this is only found in the eastern part of the State. Stone also was commonly used as a building material in this area and many of the drystone walls still stand. It is not hard to imagine scenes of torture when you are looking at Spiky Bridge, 8 km south of Swansea. Field-stones were used by convicts who built the strange structure in the 1840s.

A number of recreation areas have been developed by the Lands Department for day use along the coast, and they include Kelvedon Beach, Mayfield, Raspins and Cressy Beaches.

Swansea — oldest rural municipality

The original council chambers still are in use at Swansea, the administrative centre for the Glamorgan municipality, the oldest rural municipality in Australia. Other old buildings include the three storey Morris' General Store, run by the Morris family for more than a century, and the 1860 Community Centre, which houses a museum of local history and a superb full-sized billiard table! Visitors can play billiards or eight-ball between noon and 3.30 p.m. and from 7 to 9 p.m. Monday to Saturday.

The first hotel license was granted to the Bay View Hotel in 1840 and it still operates as an inn (in a modernised form). The waterways of Swansea are ideal for swimming, surfing, waterskiing, beach and rock fishing. An annual fishing competition each November draws competitors from near and far.

There are also facilities for golf, bowls and tennis, with accommodation in a youth hostel, motel, guest house, caravan parks (including one with a hot spa, sauna and gym), a camping ground and holiday cabins. Just out of Swansea, colonial and country accommodation are available in quaint cottages and on farms.

A good way to see Swansea buildings is to follow the town walk, which starts at the central information centre. The Schouten Gallery is worth a visit for crafts.

Travelling north, take a stop at the Swansea Bark Mill.

From bark to leather

During the Depression locals could get 6d for a bundle of black wattle bark, a basic ingredient used in tanning heavy leathers. Visitors now can watch the process (and also learn about the East Coast of the 19th century) at Australia's only restored bark mill. The mill operates on the site of a mill built in the 1890s, and its adjoining museum (with items ranging from whaling implements to a wool press built from Huon pine salvaged from an 1880 shipwreck) has won a prestigious national museum award.

The Swansea Bark Mill and East Coast Museum both feature original Oyster Bay pine posts and rafters, and, naturally, leather goods and tanned skins are among souvenirs on sale ...

Arthur Graham, a third generation member of his family in Swansea, did not collect bark during the Depression, but products of the bush helped him survive in other ways. He would hunt possums and wallabies during the game season. Competition for skins was quite fierce among buyers who would travel long distances to bargain with the hunters. Ringtail possum skins fetched two guineas a dozen but they became scarce in the 1920s as disease and hunting took their toll. Now their numbers have built up again — something that has not happened with Tasmanian tigers. Arthur's father is credited with snaring the last known tiger in the area. He caught it 10 miles out near the Campbell Town Road.

Money earned from sales of skins helped purchase crown land for ten shillings an acre, and, when Arthur wasn't working as a patrolman on the East Coast Road between Swansea and Horseshoe Bend, he was improving his sheep runs 11 miles from the township. He recalled that the introduction of bulldozers after World War II did more to change the East Coast than any other single development. Previously a stump jack was the most useful aid for clearing the land.

Transport, too, has undergone many changes since horse-drawn coaches hauled their way up from Hobart, changing horses at Buckland and Triabunna. On the Lake Leake Road to Campbell Town and the road from Colebrook to Avoca, stables were available for resting horses.

Australia's only restored bark mill is at Swansea.

The introduction of stock trucks ended the need to drive sheep long distances from markets. Arthur sometimes would spend five days on the road taking his sheep to Swansea from saleyards in Campbell Town.

Dwellings also have improved since the days when two-roomed stone huts with split paling skillions were common. Timbers were smudged over with mud, and dampness was often a problem. Building inspectors had yet to make their mark.

Cranbrook — church lives on

Like many small rural townships, Cranbrook (10 km north of Swansea) is dominatd by an historic church, the 1845 Auld Kirk, and nearby there are delightful picnic spots on the Old Coach Road. A host farm, Glen Gala, has accommodation for six people.

The turnoff to Coles Bay and the Freycinet Peninsula is a further 16 km north along the Tasman Highway. This unsealed road is often impassable after heavy rain.

Freycinet National Park

The park includes Freycinet Peninsula and Schouten Island, and it has spectacular coastal features, red granite mountains (the most famous of which are The Hazards, source of stone used in many Hobart buildings), sandy beaches and lagoons. The area is ideal for swimming, fishing, boating, waterskiing and bushwalking. it is noted for its coastal heaths, orchids, wildflowers and wide variety of birdlife (even black cockatoos and yellow wattle-birds, Australia's largest honey eater). There are large numbers of Bennetts wallabies and possums and many of them are quite tame.

Coles Bay — haven

This popular holiday resort is at the northern boundary of the National Park in one of Tasmania's most picturesque settings. Coles Bay is a good base for walks in the National Park. The walk to beautiful Wineglass Bay is most popular. The magnificent views over the bay are adequate compensation for the climb to the high point of the track.

Coles Bay has a variety of accommodation — The Chateau (units and licensed dining room), self-contained villas and cabins (sometimes with extras such as bicycles, boats, barbecue facilities and tennis courts), a camping ground, caravan park and youth hostel. Provisions can be obtained at the local store.

The Peninsula is typical of areas bestowed with names by French and Dutch explorers, and it still offers plenty of surprises for modern-day explorers ...

Freycinet Peninsula, an ideal recreation area.

Bicheno — natural and man-made attractions

This is the post-war "boom" town of the East Coast. All the motels, holiday village, stores and displays have developed in just 30 years. Named after James Ebenezer Bicheno, Colonial Secretary of Van Diemen's Land, it has long been noted for its natural splendour, including the picturesque tiny harbour called The Gulch.

Bicheno is nearly mid-way between Launceston (174 km) and Hobart (195 km). Visitors make the most of its temperate climate which provides higher average Summer temperatures than in Victoria, 750 km to the north.

When 19th century sealers and whalers used Bicheno as a base it was known as Waub's Boat Harbour. The name referred to Waubedebar, an Aboriginal woman whose grave still can be seen in the township. She became a local heroine for her part in rescuing two sealers, one of whom was her de facto husband, when they got into difficulties while fishing offshore. In 1854 Bicheno was a coal mining port, coal being brought in horse-drawn trucks along a railroad from the Denison River mines. There are remains of the convict-built bins at The Gulch which is now the centre of fish processing, crayfish and abalone industries. Diving trips are organised by the Bicheno Dive Centre, which has equipment for hire.

Bicheno has become renowned for its "cray bakes", where crayfish are cooked en-masse for parties. The town is also noted for its commercial oyster hatchery. Tiny seeds produced here are sent to nurseries and oyster farms around Australia and overseas.

Old ketch and more sealife

The oldest boat in the area is the 1902 ketch **Enterprise**, which now faces out to the seas she once plied on the timber run. Visitors to the Bicheno Sea Life Centre can go on board and see some of the memorabilia associated with her earlier days, which included a starring role in the 1926 production of the film **For the Term of his Natural Life**. Her namesake was the schooner **Enterprise** in which John Pascoe Fawkner and John Batman sailed to found the city of Melbourne.

The Sea Life Centre has aquariums with superb displays of creatures from Tasmania's coast. There are giant crabs from the continental shelf, crayfish, enormous conger eels, sea horses, abalone and hundreds of scale fish. An audio-visual presentation tells the story of the Tasmanian fishing industry. Fairy penguins are one of the outdoor attractions. There's a coffee

Creatures of the day — and night

Pelicans, emus, rainbow lorikeets, rare and territorial birds are just a few of the species that can be seen at the East Coast Bird and Wildlife Park just north of Bicheno. The Park has an excellent picnic or barbecue area, and a small train takes passengers round the 35 ha. if you don't feel like walking. Stops are made at feeding areas (watch out for those pelicans!), and at the walk-through aviary. Heading north the highway passes numerous picnic areas (including the Douglas River) and, after the "haul" up Elephant Pass, it is worth stopping at the French Tea House for pancakes and other light snacks.

A new scenic road links Falmouth and Chain of Lagoons, to the south. A walking track leads south from the Bicheno blowhole around the coast to Cape Lodi, returning along the ridgetops. The walk takes about six hours.

Lorikeets feed at the East Coast Bird and Wildlife Park.

The Enterprise takes a well-earned "rest".

St Marys — junction

Passengers travelling to the East Coast by rail used to welcome the sight of St Marys, and the "end of the line". Now, however, it is used only by freight trains.

St Marys is at the junction of the Tasman Highway and the Esk Main Road, which leads to the Midland Highway. It is a centre for dairying, pastoral and timber industries, and has shops, a hotel and camping area, plus a homely youth hostel on a farm 5 km away at German Town.

Fingal — coal and whisky!

The headquarters of the Tasmanian coal industry is at Fingal, 21 km inland from St Mary. Each year visitors travel from throughout the State and beyond for coal shovelling championships. This was also where the State's first payable gold was found in 1852.

The Fingal Hotel, built in 1850 as the Talbot Arms, is home to a collection of hundreds of brands of Scotch whisky. Malahide, a National Trust classified homestead, is not open to the public.

Avoca — mining base

Avoca, midway between Fingal and the Midlands Highway, also serves the mining areas of Rossarden and Story's Creek. Homes such as "Bona Vista" reflect the rise and fall of fortunes, the magnificence of the 1848 building now but a memory. It can be inspected by arrangement with the caretaker.

Mathinna — falls and superb trees

A Forestry Reserve is located 24 km north of Fingal at Mathinna, once the destination of gold diggers. It was named after an Aboriginal girl "taken in" by Lady Franklin, wife of an early Tasmanian Governor, who wanted to prove that the natives could adjust to the European society. The reserve included the majestic Mathinna Falls.

The Evercreech Forest Reserve, to the north east, has a 300 year old white gum, the tallest of its species in the State. With three other gums it forms a group known as the White Knights — similar to Western Australia's Four Aces ...

North of St Marys the Tasman Highway goes through St Marys Pass Reserve, one of the few areas where Tasmanian ironbark is found.

Falmouth — duck shooting

Falmouth lies at the foot of St Marys Pass, 4 km from the highway. The small township is noted for its beaches, fishing grounds and duck shooting. In Falmouth there are holiday cottages and at a holiday village, 9 km south along a coastal gravel road, the emphasis is on family activities. Here there are self-contained units, games rooms, a pool, canoe lake, tennis courts, golf course and children's pony rides. Stores can be bought from a kiosk and there are miles of sandy beaches where you feel you are the only person on earth.

Scamander — fishermens' mecca

The Scamander River is well known for its bream and trout — fishermen line the bridge while others try their luck from boats. Sea and beach fishing are also popular and it's not only the fish who take to the water!

Scamander has a motel, holiday unit and cottage accommodation, a caravan and camping area with its own swimming pool, a youth hostel and a licensed restaurant.

Beaumaris — scenery and sport

There are magnificent coastal views from a forest reserve which adjoins the beaches and lagoons at Beaumaris, 5 km north of Scamander. The area is ideal for water sports and fishing, and there is a motel, licensed restaurant, and small golf course. Surfboards, fishing gear and golf clubs are available for hire.

St Helens — fishermen, tourists and more!

St Helens was settled in 1830 and 40 years later became the service centre for the tin mining fields at Blue Tiers and Lottah. It is the largest town on the East Coast and is a base for fishing fleets (crayfish, scallops, abalone and scalefish), timber milling, mineral and dairying industries, as well as tourism.

Visitors are well catered for with a variety of accommodation (hotels, motels, guest houses, holiday units, caravan parks and camping grounds), licensed and unlicensed restaurants, full shopping and sporting facilities, and vehicle hire (even bicycles!). Professional fishermen are not the only ones who favour St Helens. Fishing is the main recreation in Georges Bay, on which the town is situated, and charter boats are available for off-shore game fishing. St Helens has a game fishing club and its members will be happy to offer advice.

The town has a museum and history room, and a plant nursery — appropriate for a district noted for its wildflowers, especially orchids. The bay, estuaries and lagoons are good for bird watching.

St Helens is a useful base for visiting a number of other attractions in the area. Binalong Bay is a particularly scenic beach resort 11 km to the north and there are picturesque drives to the State recreation areas at St Helens Point and Humbug Point, and to Stieglitz and Sloop Reef on the coast.

St Columba Falls.

From St Helens the Tasman Highway winds westwards via Goulds Country to Pyengana, 27 km away. Here there is an unusual refreshment stop — the Pub in the Paddock (quite true to its name!).

Trout fisherman can try their luck in the North and South George Rivers and at the St Columba Falls State Reserve, 8 km from Pyengana on the South George Road. The focal point in the reserve are the 110 m high falls set amid lush fern gullies.

"A celestial's home."

Weldborough — Chinese left their mark

The Weldborough Pass provides spectacular mountain scenery on the eastern approach to Weldborough (midway between St Helens and Scottsdale).

Hundreds of Chinese people came to Tasmania during the tin mining boom last century and many made Weldborough their base. They retained their own culture and lifestyles, and brought with them some of their more precious possessions, including a Joss House that is now restored and displayed at the Queen Victoria Museum and Art Gallery in Launceston. It was presented by Chinese families who had lived in the North East, and some of the Joss House pieces are considered finer than those of the wealthiest Hong Kong temples. No expense was spared and there was extensive use of gold leaf ...

Bill Goss was one of the last of Weldborough's packers. These men used pack horses to carry stores and equipment out to miners' camps and returned with the tin. Bill recalled details of one particular Chinese family. Mr Chin sent home to China for a pure Chinese (not Mandarin) bride, and paid £600 to bring her to Tasmania. She was not allowed out in Weldborough until she had produced a son. Mr Chin was "head" of the Chinese in the town, but when his son duly arrived his wife became boss of the household!

Bill's load sometimes included the town drunks whom he would pack back to their huts — armed with as many bottles of "pain killers" as they could carry. Problems of over-indulgence were common. Many of the prospectors would spend weeks at a time at their diggings, then head to town to unwind — often for days on end. The hotel had large stables and the dung heap often formed a bed for the drunks who found it a good spot to keep warm ... Now the local watering hole is described by its owners as "The worst pub on the coast". It's up

to visitors to decide, however, if they really are eating possum pie, Tasmanian devil or witchety grubs!

At Moorina, 11 km north of Weldborough, there is an interesting Chinese section in the cemetery. Offerings of food were left for the spirits of the dead at an altar and conical oven. The body would be buried with a pair of shoes to "help them on their journey".

The tin mining towns of Pioneer and Gladstone are reached by a secondary road which heads north from the Tasman Highway just past Moorina.

Gladstone — tin and gems

Gladstone is one of the few North East towns still relying on tin. It is also noted for its geological formations and is the haunt of lapidarists. Boobyalla is among the once sub-stantial towns that have now disappeared. A visit to the site, north-east of Gladstone, reveals just a few remains of buildings and the cemetery. The pervading stillness is typical of ghost towns in the area.

An unsealed road leads to Eddystone Point and the Eddystone Light (built in 1887). It forms the most eastern point of the Tasmanian mainland. There are camping facilities near Eddystone Point, but campers should take their own water supplies.

Mt William National Park — wildlife reserve

The Mt William National Park has an abundance of native animals and is a sanctuary for Tasmania's only kangaroos, the Forester, and the rare New Holland mouse. The park is home to more than half Tasmania's species of vertebrates. Coastal heaths are a feature and there are good swimming and fishing spots.

The Tasman Highway continues from Moorina to Scottsdale, the main North East town, and on to Launceston, Tasmania's second city.

Launceston

Australia's third oldest city, Launceston, lies on the Tamar River nestled in valleys and surrounded by mountains. Bass and Flinders discovered the Tamar estuary in 1798 while they were trying to determine whether Van Diemen's Land was joined to the rest of Australia.

In 1804 Lieutenant-Colonel William Paterson led an expedition from New South Wales to establish a settlement. He landed where George Town now stands near the mouth of the Tamar, and took possession of Port Dalrymple.

Launceston, originally called Patersonia, was founded a year later, and the first shelters and buildings were between the Cataract Gorge and what is now City Park. Its name was changed soon afterwards to Launceston, in honour of Governor King — he was born in Launceston, a town settled a thousand years before on the Tamar River in Cornwall. Strong ties have been retained by the two Launcestons. The Tasmanian city has also initiated official sister city relationships with centres in other countries, notably Japan.

Launceston has earned its title of "Garden City", and numerous well-established parks and gardens provide areas for relaxation and botanic studies. Early industries in Launceston and its surrounds concentrated on subsistence — crops and flour milling —but a number soon turned their attention to brewing. For some, especially the military, a plentiful supply of liquor was regarded as important as food. Spirits were imported from England and rum from the West Indies. Fermented liquors were considered safer than the often turgid waters of the North Esk from where domestic water was drawn.

Launceston, the State's second city, always has been the geographic and commercial hub of northern and midland Tasmania, and its importance as a distribution centre has increased over the years.

But the face of commerce has changed. Sir Raymond Ferrall, whose links with Launceston extend back to 1853 when his grandfather was a carpenter, has seen a number of the changes.

Early this century he watched his father's grocery and wholesale business expand and later spent some years as a commercial traveller for the firm — buying anything "from cricket balls to sponge cakes". One of the features of Launceston between 1900 and 1920 was the large number of livery stables. This reflected its development as a marketing centre and country people would come to town on Tuesdays and Thursdays in their horse-drawn vehicles. While they went about their business horses were stabled and fed.

There were six grain and chaff merchants in Launceston, and other thriving businesses centred on milling and bread-making. Bread from about 30 bakeries was delivered in gaily painted carts, fancy fringed cotton coverings keeping sun off the loaves. Work was plentiful for a dozen boot and shoe makers, and barbers also did a roaring trade. At times up to 50 mugs and brushes were lined up as barbers prepared to shave their customers for 3d!

Sir Raymond recalled the closure of factories which specialised in items as diverse as shirts, biscuits, soap, paint, hats and liqueurs —all as a result of increased competition from large companies.

Steamers used to travel up the Tamar River and Sir Raymond, a former master warden for the port, observed all the changes as roll-on/roll-off cargo ferries took over the interstate run, and Bell Bay developed as the terminal.

Orcharding has declined in the Tamar area, but an exciting future seems to lie ahead for new ventures involving grape growing — part of the "new face" ...

Throughout all the changes Launceston has retained a quiet charm that is reflected in its old homes, churches, commercial buildings and parks. The best way to get round the city area is by foot — at every turn there are reminders of the past.

Brisbane Street, Launceston, circa 1867.

A heritage of buildings

Macquarie House in the City Square was built in 1830 as a warehouse for merchant Henry Reed who was associated with the founding of Melbourne. Later it was military barracks and an office building and now, following a mammoth restoration programme, it houses a section of the Queen Victoria Museum and Art Gallery and a restaurant. Macquarie House is open daily (afternoons only at weekends).

Shrimps Restaurant in George Street was in turn china, novelty and shoe stores, and the original building, built in 1824, was a favourite haunt of martial music composer, Alex Lithgow, known as the Sousa of the antipodes.

An art school now flourishes in the York Street building occupied by the Union Brewery and later famous as Thyne Brothers Knitting Mill.

Macquarie House has a new role.

National Trust contribution

Shott's Umbrella Shop in George Street is the last genuine period shop in Tasmania. Three generations of the Shott family operated the blackwood lined store and a selection of their umbrellas still is displayed. The shop is preserved by the National Trust which uses it as an information centre and gift store.

The Trust also bought Staffordshire House in Charles Street, believed to be the only Georgian merchant's home remaining in Australia.

Joss House — a museum feature

The Queen Victoria Museum and Art Gallery in Wellington Street was built late last century and it retains the splendour of the period, both inside and out. A major attraction is the Chinese Joss House given by Chinese families who lived in north eastern Tasmania. It came from Weldborough, where it was the world's southernmost working joss house. Gold leaf is used extensively on fans, lanterns and wall signs, and there are joss sticks, weapons (including an executioner's sword) and puppet house.

The Museum and Art Gallery has a unique collection of Tasmanian fauna, Aborigine and penal settlement relics, and colonial paintings. There are regular public viewings at a planetarium which features the southern night sky.

The museum is open daily (afternoon only on Sunday) except Christmas Day and Good Friday.

Churches large and small

Launceston's many lovely churches include a synagogue built in 1844 in St John Street. It is one of only two synagogues remaining from colonial times.

St John's Church near Princes Square has a Georgian tower which was completed in 1830 as a part of the original church. John Batman, the founder of Melbourne, was married in St John's.

The Pilgrim Uniting Church in Paterson Street has sections dating from 1835. The building has been adapted to meet its new role as the Launceston central parish; modern materials have been used in a traditional style in the cloisters which form a walkway between city areas.

Squares, parks and gardens

Princes Square, once a brick field, features a bronze fountain bought at the 1858 Paris Exhibition. In the early 1800s the square was used for political meetings and even a hot air ballooning attempt. It was also the site for the hanging of two bushrangers. One of the oak trees in the square was planted by the Duke of Edinburgh in 1868.

Another focal point is the fountain at the busy intersection of High Street and Elphin Road. It was used for watering horses and dogs and the elaborate cast iron structure originally incorporated a street lamp.

The fountain forms a focal point in City Park.

A joss house is a legacy of Chinese settlers.

A city haven

City Park dates back to the late 1820s and has appeal for people of all ages.

Children clamber over a cannon (bearing a Russian inscription which is more than 140 years old), and on an A4 locomotive (built in Manchester in 1891). The locomotive "retired" in 1951. On three occasions it had Royal parties among its passengers.

A zoological section was established late last century, and wallabies and ducks now have been joined by some newcomers — monkeys, which live in specially designed quarters that should make them the envy of their counterparts in the "free world".

Albert Hall, on the edge of the park, was built in 1891 for the Tasmanian International Exhibition and features a magnificent water organ.

The John Hart Conservatory, noted for its native and exotic species of flora, presents a blaze of colour to brighten even the dullest day.

Arts, crafts and commerce

The Design Centre of Tasmania (adjacent to the City Park) has displays of design work by the State's top artists and craftsmen (open daily but closed on Saturday afternoon and Sunday morning).

Ritchie's Flour Mill now houses an arts centre. The four-level complex, built in 1845 includes a quaint Georgian miller's cottage — now serving as tearooms.

Wool is a popular material for craftwork, but at the Waverley Woollen Mills it is important on a much larger scale. Established in 1874 this is Australia's oldest woollen mill, and it is open for inspection daily until 4 p.m. The mill is in Waverley Road, 5 km from the city centre, and visitors can watch the entire production process — from greasy wool to finished items such as blankets, fashion garments and accessories, and even genuine tartans! An 1889 hydro electric generator is among historic plant equipment on display, and examples of goods produced at the mill are on sale in a showroom which is open from 9 to 5 daily.

The National Automobile Museum of Tasmania adjoins the mills. It's open daily, and exhibits range from a 1909 BSA car to a modern Ferrari Boxer.

Cloth and socks

The Tamar Knitting Mills in Hobart Road were once Australia's largest manufacturer of lambswool garments. Visitors can see yarn being knitted into cloth and a process whereby the famous Tasmanian hikers' greasy wool socks are knitted on coarse-gauge hosiery machines. Factory inspections are Monday to Friday, while a shop with goods produced at the mills is also open on Saturday morning.

Work of craftsman Les Blakebrough.

Huon pine bowls made by Merv Gray.

Visitors can inspect the Waverley Woollen Mills.

Launceston Federal Country Club Casino.

Inns of old — and a casino

Launceston has a full range of accommodation, vehicle hire restaurants, shopping, sporting and convention facilities.

Historical establishments such as the Colonial Motor Inn (built in 1847 — as the Launceston Grammar School) and the Batman-Fawkner Inn (whose first landlord, John Fawkner, planned the settlement which grew into Melbourne) contrast with modern complexes such as the Launceston Federal Country Club Casino.

Situated 10 km from the city centre at Prospect, it is Tasmania's second casino. The 85 ha site includes an 18 hole golf course, picturesque ornamental lake and horse riding, tennis and squash facilities. Indoors there is a pool, sauna and spa, lavish dining areas, a galleried cabaret room for staging floorshows and performances by leading artists, a discotheque, luxury accommodation and a convention centre.

Try your luck

At the casino itself, traditional games such as roulette and blackjack are joined by the not-so-traditional two-up. Since it opened in 1982 the complex has given a significant boost to the Launceston entertainment scene. It is open seven days a week till the wee small hours of the morning ...

Tasmania's newest deluxe hotel, the Launceston International, has a selection of bars and dining areas. Function and convention facilities are centred around a large, rectangular ballroom, and, when it's time to unwind, there are spa pools, a sauna and massage room.

Lavish floorshows are among casino entertainments.

Penny Royal — a new world

The massive Penny Royal development is built on the past, but has a rosy future. It started with the re-building of an 1825 cornmill, moved stone by stone from Cressy. Soon there were examples of millwright, blacksmith and wheelwright shops, a museum and gift shop.

Now visitors from throughout Australia and overseas are attracted to this world of gunpowder mills, windmill and old-time transport — including a paddle steamer, children's steam railway, an Edwardian tram, a 10 gun sloop (with cannon that visitors can fire), a cutter which calls at an underground armoury magazine, a jail and gunners' quarters. Also on display are cannons salvaged from Horatio Nelson's favourite 74 gun man o'war, the **Collosus**, which sank when it was hit by a hurricane near the Scilly Isles at the beginning of the 18th century.

The mills, foundry and fort are set in an old quarry, and waterfalls which flow into lakes are among "hazards" faced during barge rides around the complex to the cavern of the Powderkeg Restaurant. For those who are reluctant to leave this magical setting there is luxury motel-type accommodation (complete with tavern) plus self-contained family units, named after British officers such as Captain Mostyn and Captain Younghead who were killed in a bloody battle against Zulus.

New life for an 1825 cornmill.

Penny Royal Gunpowder Mill — another world.

Lady Stelfox at the Cataract Gorge.

Paddle steamer days relived

For another journey back in time take the paddle steamer, **Lady Stelfox**, which leaves Ritchie's landing stage, near the Penny Royal, five times daily. During a 40 minute cruise up the Cataract Gorge and around the harbour travellers can view workings of the Huon pine boat, which has the only known walking beam engine of its type. Refreshments are served on board and there is a licensed bar.

Cataract Gorge — a century of visitors

Few places could have an attraction like the Cataract Gorge within 10 minutes walking distance of the city. Almost vertical cliffs line the banks where the South Esk cataract enters the Tamar River. The gorge still retains the wild beauty that impressed its first European visitors during exploration of the Tamar in 1804.

The Cliff Grounds and a recreation area on the opposite side, known as the First Basin, are linked by a suspension bridge and a chairlift, which has a 308 m span — the longest single chairlift span in the world. Extensive gardens at the Cliff Ground include nature trails, a Fairy Dell, complete with peacocks, a Victorian style band rotunda, and a licensed restaurant which serves excellent luncheons, morning and afternoon teas, and light refreshments. Canoes are available for hire.

Power and recreation

A path leads farther up the South Esk to the Duck Reach hydro electric power station, the first in the southern hemisphere. It is now superseded by the Trevallyn station at the Trevallyn Dam, which can be visited from 8.30 a.m. to 4.30 p.m. on weekdays and between 10 a.m. and 6 p.m. at weekends. The Lands Department has developed this area for recreation activities including swimming, windsurfing, boating and waterskiing.

This is one of a number of pleasant picnic spots available in Launceston. Another is the Punchbowl Reserve, which has barbecue facilities and is near a wildlife sanctuary and zoo, and a magnificent rhododendron garden.

A traveller's base

Launceston is the northern gateway to Tasmania and also a base for tours to the North East, North West, and Midlands. Scenic flights can be made in light planes from Launceston Airport, and a charter boat for cruising and fishing is based at Blackwall on the Tamar River. Coaches and mini-coaches make trips round the city and farther afield, and charter transport is available for bushwalkers wanting to explore the wilderness regions of the State.

Launceston presents a pleasant blend of Georgian, Italienate, Victorian and Edwardian buildings and modern man-made developments such as the Yorktown and Quadrant shopping centres, the Country Club Casino, and the Tasmanian Silverdome – the biggest indoor sports arena in Australia.

It offers something for everyone ...

Launceston — growth of Tasmania's second city.

North and North East

Early last century Launceston was a base for explorers, prospectors, settlers and adventurers as they headed west along the coast and inland to exploit the rich soils of the North West, east to seek their fortunes from the mineral and timber riches of the North East, and south to what has become one of Tasmania's richest farming regions. Fine roads now link areas where pack horses once carted goods along narrow tracks. Rubble is all that remains of many settlements, but, amidst the modern developments, it is still possible to recapture some of the atmosphere of those past days.

For our part we shall now explore the west and east Tamar regions, the North East as far as Derby and Winnaleah, and west to Deloraine.

The Tamar River runs 64 km from the confluence of the North Esk and South Esk Rivers to Bass Strait, and the estuary provides Australia's longest navigable inland waterway for ships up to 4,000 tonnes.

The West Tamar Highway travels through the Launceston suburbs of Trevallyn and Riverside on to Legana, scene of an ambitious Swiss village development and a base for visits to the Notley Fern Gorge. Tasmania has developed an international reputation for its wines. At St Matthias Vineyard at Rosevears it's possible to taste and buy a variety of the best wines.

Carting hay, circa 1920.

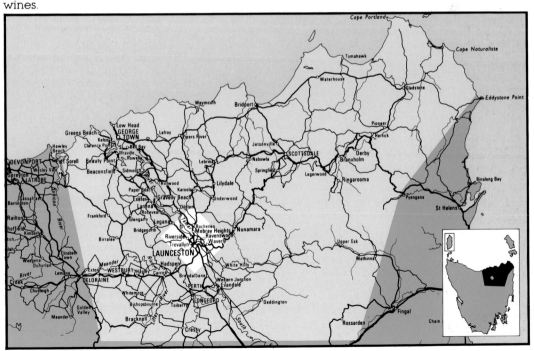

Grindelwald — touch of Switzerland

A Swiss style village in Upper Craythorne Road has privately owned redwood and cedar chalets, a chapel, trout-filled lake, tearooms and a restaurant.

Notley Hill — ferns and wildlife

Colonial timber cutters removed much of the forest in this district. However, at Notley Fern Gorge, 23 km from Launceston via Legana, there is a remnant of the heavy rainforest. Its trees, ferns and shrubs provide a sanctuary for wildlife.

Early last century this was bushranger territory, with forests providing cover for Matthew Brady and his colleagues. Just north of Legana there is a lookout where he checked on the movement of troops and potential "clients". Brady eventually was captured and was hanged in Hobart in 1826.

As well as vineyards, Rosevears has a traditional ale brewery in the historic pub, and a sanctuary for marine birds. The Waterbird Haven Trust is open on the first Sunday of each month.

Exeter — rural base

Exeter (24 km from Launceston) is a base for the West Tamar farming and orcharding industries, and has a hotel with accommodation, counter meals, a restaurant and shops. Souvenirs and crafts are available. Pottery is a speciality.

Near here are the river resorts of Blackwell, Paper Beach and Gravelly Beach.

Oysters tempt palates

Just off the highway at Deviot is an important oyster farm. For years this was the only place in Tasmania where oysters were cultivated, but now there are more than 30 commercial oyster farms around the State. Their products are developing an enviable reputation throughout Australian and overseas. Farmers use traditional stick-growing methods as well as the new basket and mesh systems.

Batman Bridge — engineering masterpiece

The Batman Bridge crosses the Tamar 30 km downstream from Launceston. The bridge is dominated by a 100 m high steel A-frame tower. Along the bank nearby there are picnic grounds with barbecue and toilet facilities. Opened in 1968, it was one of the world's first cable-stayed truss bridges and it provided the first permanent crossing of the Tamar River.

Farther north on the western side are the townships of Sidmouth, Beaconsfield, Beauty Point, Kelso and Green's Beach.

Sidmouth — Auld Kirk

A small church at Sidmouth (36 km from Launceston) has had varied "fortunes" since it was built by convicts and free labour in 1846. It remained derelict for some years after a fire in 1900, but now has been restored. Tourist information is available in Sidmouth.

Beaconsfield — golden history

The quiet 19th century agricultural township of Beaconsfield (one named Cabbage Tree Hill) took on a new lease of life in 1869 with the discovery of gold. The area boomed for more than 40 years, with over $6 million worth of gold being extracted before water seepage forced the mine to close. In recent years there has been further exploration to see if any workable gold deposits still exist near Beaconsfield. The Grubb Shaft Museum, open from Tuesday to Sunday, is in a restored mine building.

An insight into the past is given at a replica of a miner's abode and at the Flowery Gully School exhibit. The old school has been restored and it again has the atmosphere of the early 1900s — it is complete with original five-place Baltic pine desks. The school is open by appointment and represents a fine example of community groups working on a project for the benefit of the town and its visitors.

York Town near Beaconsfield was the site of settlement in 1804, and a memorial and commemorative stone have been built adjacent to the York Town Rivulet.

Beaconsfield gold mine.

Beauty Point — maritime college

Originally Beauty Point was the port for Beaconsfield's gold mining industry. The berths at Inspection Head now have freezer, cool store and bulk tallow facilities.

However, in recent times, development has centred around the establishment of the Australian Maritime College's base for its practical seamanship and fisheries training. Another campus of the college is at Newnham near Launceston, site of the major academic buildings and specialist laboratories. Students come from all over Australia and the Pacific Basin for full and part-time marine education.

Beauty Point has excellent launching ramps and a marina, and this is a popular fishing and aquatic centre. It has hotel, motel, caravan park and camping facilities.

Fishing and beaches

An ABC radio transmitting mast is a landmark at Kelso, 54 km from Launceston. During its heyday in the 1830s Kelso was the western terminus for a punt carrying livestock and goods to the North West from Launceston, via George Town, but now it is a holiday and fishing resort, with caravan and camping areas.

Green's Beach, at the mouth of the Tamar, is one of the traditional beach resorts of northern Tasmania. It has a store, caravan and camping areas, and a golf course, and stands at the eastern end of the Asbestos Range National Park which extends to Port Sorell (see page 64).

When travelling along the East Tamar Highway, which runs from Launceston to George Town and on to Low Head, tourists get splendid panoramic views of the Tamar Valley. Low Head has always been an important navigation station and as early as 1825 a signalling system connected Low Head and Launceston to advise on shipping movements.

Dilston — residential
Development has taken a different turn at Dilston (14 km from Launceston) than that envisaged when coal was discovered in the 1880s. Money invested in building jetties and opening up seams was lost when the coal turned out to be an inferior type of lignite. Nevertheless, some buildings have survived — the 1834 inn is now an antique shop. Dilston is a favoured residential area for "out of town" living — something which Tasmania offers within very short distances of its main cities.

Windermere — church "for cameras"
Pioneer settler Dr Matthias Gaunt used his land grant for purposes which ranged from milling and grape-growing to church-building! St Matthias Church (20 km from Launceston) was erected in 1842 and it is the oldest in Australia with a history of continuous use. Dr Gaunt's grave is among those in the historic cemetery. The church in its postcard-type setting among trees is a popular subject for photographers. People can fish from a nearby jetty and there is also a boat launching ramp at Windermere, which is a short distance off the highway.

Hillwood — strawberries
Hillwood is a fruit growing area. Visitors can pick their own strawberries and other berry fruits during the season between November and April.

A steam locomotive is a feature in a playground area and Hillwood is a good spot for fishing.

Just past a junction with the road leading from the Batman Bridge is a roadside sanctuary on the way to Bell Bay.

Bell Bay — industry and trade
In 1947 it was announced that Australia's first aluminium industry would be established in the Launceston area, and Bell Bay was chosen as the site. Developers had to ensure that natural beauty of the surroundings would be preserved as far as possible.

The Vaccuum Oil Company and Australian Aluminium Commission (now Comalco) established operations at Bell Bay in 1950, and were joined later by a subsidiary of the Broken Hill Company, Temco.

A new terminal was built in 1958 when Bell Bay became the base for services of the Australian National Line's roll-on/roll-off cargo ferry trade.

Tasmania's first thermal power station, commissioned in 1971, is near Bell Bay, and the area also has been selected for woodchip operations.

The Comalco plant is open for inspection on Thursdays at 2 p.m. (but no children under 14 are allowed, and visitors should wear trousers or slacks and strong shoes). Group tours can be made at other times by arrangement.

St Matthias Church, Windermere.

Heading for home, on the Tamar River.

George Town — preserving the past

Developments in George Town in the past few years have aimed at preserving the town's history — and that goes back a long way. Europeans first landed here in 1804 when a gale stranded H.M.S. **Buffalo**. The first permanent settlement was established in 1811.

A monument on the Esplanade marks the spot where the crew of the **Buffalo** landed, and a short distance away in the town centre, a former Watch House (built in 1843) has been restored as a folk museum. The building has served as a doctor's surgery, shops and council chambers. The latest additions have included a toilet block for the disabled. The museum is open daily from 11 a.m. to 3 p.m.

The Grove, formerly the port officer's residence, now opens its doors to visitors each day. Grove maids serve refreshments, and locally produced handcrafts and souvenirs are on sale.

St Mary Magdalen Church of England and its graveyard are worth a visit.

George Town is the residential centre for employees at Bell Bay, and has shops, restaurants, hotel, motel, caravan and camping facilities. The **Furneaux Explorer** sets out from here or from Beauty Point each Monday for a four-day cruise of the Furneaux Islands.

Low Head — maritime importance

Low Head is at the mouth of the Tamar on the eastern shore, and the pilot station is one of the oldest in Australia. The original lighthouse was built in the 1830s, but the present structure dates from 1889.

The pilot station has been restored by the Port of Launceston Authority and now houses a maritime museum, where exhibits include station logs from 1859, old diving equipment and items salvaged from wrecked boats — even full bottles of beer, castor oil and mustard! It can be inspected by arrangement with the Authority.

Low Head is noted for its surf and lagoon beaches.

The North East is traversed by roads (of varying qualities) which give opportunities for many round trips.

The major link is the Tasman Highway which crosses from the East Coast through the forests of the North East and on to Launceston. Another main route runs from Bell Bay along the northern coast.

Scottsdale, on the Tasman Highway, is also the junction for a road from the resort town of Bridport on the coast, and for an inland road which reaches Launceston by way of Lilydale.

From Bell Bay there is a minor road leading to the old mining town of Lefroy, now a virtual ghost town. Mine workings and brick ruins are all that remain of this once bustling area which reached a peak of activity during the gold rush era of the 1870s.

Wine brings acclaim

Pipers River, 36 km from George Town, is in a farming district which is now the centre of attention as a grape-growing area. Vineyards near here have produced award-winning table wines that are keenly sought by experts who recognise the potential of Tasmania's product.

The cool climate is ideal for growing grapes, and the aim is to produce wine with a distinctive Tasmanian quality. In the past 25 years the industry has developed from its initial experimental stages to a point where wines are exported to traditional wine-producing countries such as Germany.

Low Head lighthouse.

Weymouth — waterskiing

Waterskiing is popular at the resort of Weymouth, 14 km off the main road. It is one of numerous places along the coast named after centres in the English county of Dorset.

Bridport — fish exports

Holidaymakers flock to Bridport, 85 km from Launceston. Its beaches and waterways provide outlets for all forms of aquatic reaction, and accommodation includes well-developed camping and caravan areas. Crayfish tails for the lucrative American market are among seafoods processed at a Bridport factory, which is open for inspection by arrangement.

Bridport used to be a port for timber which was brought by rail from a mill 16 km away. Now it is a residential area for many people who work at George Town and Scottsdale, and for a number of "retirees" ...

Ernie Armstrong moved here in 1981 from Winnaleah, but for decades most of the North East was his "haunt". In his early years he lived in many parts of the State, including Middleton, Waterloo, York Plains and St Marys.

Ernie is typical of the people who can't resist doing the odd bit of prospecting in the North East. With a friend he spent many weekends searching for uranium — and they actually found some! The Commonwealth Government paid a £50 reward, but that was the end of the story because the rich Mary Kathleen deposits had just been discovered, and they offered a more promising future.

Old tin mines dot the North East and they are a good source of stones for lapidarists. Quartz crystals (smoky and clear), agates and jasper are among finds Ernie made around Gladstone. During the war years crystals from the region were used by the military for making prisms for microscopes, field glasses and telescopes. Ernie remembered how smoky quartz was put in a coal fire and covered with clay. The heat used to turn the quartz clear.

Most of the old tin prospectors have gone nowadays, but timber production still is important in areas such as Scottsdale and Branxholm.

Field naturalists, like Ernie, find Bridport a fruitful exploration ground, especially for native orchids. Along the coast the road continues 26 km to Waterhouse and on to Gladstone (see page 44). Secondary roads lead to unspoilt beaches, fishing waters and a river reserve at Tomahawk.

A scenic route from Launceston leaves suburban Rocherlea and continues to Turner's Marsh (pheasant farm), Karoola and Lalla.

Karoola — steam engines
Steam enthusiasts spend hours of leisure time working on their pride and joy, a 1912 Marshall portable steam engine, and other steam equipment being restored at Karoola. Near here there is a host farm, The Stonehouse, which is noted for its cattle and organically grown vegetables.

Lalla — bountiful produce
Lalla, 25 km from Launceston, is a good spot for people who like things from "mother earth". A weekend market in The Appleshed has locally grown fruit and vegetables, honey, plants, and art and crafts.

The W.A.G. Walker Rhododendron Reserve, administered by the Lands Department, has the greatest variety of rhododendrons in the southern hemisphere. There are barbecue facilities. Check opening times.

Handcraft enthusiasts can stock up on weaving and yarn supplies at the Woolshed.

Lilydale — waterfalls and famous oaks
Two oak trees on a reserve 3 km from Lilydale's town centre were grown from acorns sent from Great Windsor Park and planted on Coronation Day in 1936. Short walks lead to two waterfalls. The reserve has a pleasant picnic area with shelters, fireplaces, coin-operated barbecues, toilets, water and free camping facilities (although there is a charge for showers and power connection).

Stores in Lilydale (27 km from Launceston) include ones stocking lavender products, for which the district is famous. The local tavern has discos on Friday and Saturday night.

Bushwalkers use Lilydale as a base when heading to Mt Arthur, and a road leads south to Underwood (where there is an apiary) and the turnoff to Hollybank Forest Reserve.

Sawmill operations at Lilydale.

No racquets now
Past owners of the 70 ha Hollybank Reserve included the Alexander Patent Racquet Company, who believed it was an ideal location for production of English ash trees for use in timber tennis racquets. However the trees grew too slowly and the venture failed. Now it is a study area for Launceston schools and a peaceful place for walks and picnics. The reserve has barbecue facilities.

Nabowla — sweet smell of success
Lavender grown at Nabowla (54 km from Launceston) is famous world-wide. The Bridestowe Lavender Farm, one of the largest producers of flower oil for European and American perfumeries, is open for inspection between Boxing Day and the third week in January, when flowers are in bloom and fields are a mass of mauve. There are picnic areas and a souvenir kiosk. Mint grown at Nabowla is used for flavouring confectionery, toothpaste and medicines. The essential oils industry seems to have a promising future in Tasmania.

The road leads on to Scottsdale and a return trip to Launceston can be made on either the Tasman Highway or via Bridport and the East Tamar.

Nabowla and Lilydale are famous for lavender products.

Much of the 63 km journey from Launceston to Scottsdale is on winding road but there is ample compensation in the magnificent forest and farmland scenery. Massive ferns come right to the roadside and the view from the Sideling Lookout is memorable.

A turnoff 28 km from Launceston leads to the access road for Mt Barrow (1,415 m). National and commercial television transmitters for northern Tasmania are sited on the mountain, which forms part of an area noted for its alpine vegetation. Mt Barrow is near the Ben Lomond National Park and skiing slopes, 61 km from Launceston, but the best access to the Park is on roads leading south from Launceston, then eastwards (see page 32) ...

Myrtle Park — picnic spot
Mt Arthur forms a dramatic backdrop to Myrtle Park, 33 km from Launceston. A feature in this farming and timber area is a large recreation ground by St Patrick's River, a good spot for picnics and there is a kiosk at the site. Fresh produce often can be bought from roadside sellers on the way to Scottsdale, the "capital" of the North East.

Scottsdale — busy centre
This is the main town in North East Tasmania and services a rich agricultural district and timber and food processing industries. It was named after Government surveyor James Scott, who, in the 1850s, was one of the first Europeans to tackle the region's virgin bush.

Scottsdale has a full range of shops (including antiques) and sporting amenities. Former prosperity was based on mining and timber, and the pine industry still is important.

Tonganah, 7 km away, is the site of a particle board mill and large hop-growing operations. The Australian headquarters of the Army Food Research Laboratories is at Scottsdale, and the town also has a processing factory specialising in deep freezing and dehydration of vegetables.

Farming is mainly dairying and cash crops (especially vegetables). Scottsdale has a hotel and motel, and caravan and camping facilities.

Branxholm — agriculture replaces tin
There are extensive pine plantations near Branxholm, 90 km from Launceston and 75 km from St Helens, and activities in the town include milling and hop growing. Tin used to be important, but agricultural production now is the main source of income. A Forestry Commission fire tower on Mt Horror can be inspected during the Summer. Branxholm has a motel, caravan and camping park.

Ringarooma — dairy district
Ringarooma is off the main highway 21 km from Scottsdale. Late last century gold was discovered at nearby Alberton, but this centre is now deserted. Farming and forestry, with the associated milling operations, are the main industries.

Beyond Ringarooma other attractions include Mathinna Hill (panoramic views) and Legerwood, base of the North Eastern Co-operative Dairy Society butter factory and a timber mill. The Ringarooma River and Cascade Frome Dam have good fishing. The hydro scheme at the dam is unusual because it is privately owned, the Hydro Electric Commission buying power produced by the company. The scheme has been in operation for more than 80 years, and it was 40 years before any bearings had to be replaced in the German made generator.

Agriculture is growing in importance in the North East.

Derby — tin still important

Once a lively tin mining town with the industry based on the famous Breisis Mine, Derby (104 km from Launceston, 66 km from St Helens) has turned back the clock to create a modern attraction! The old Derby School now houses a mine museum and visitors can take a trip to the Shanty Town Tin Mine and see how it was done in the "good old days". Hearty miners' lunches are among fare at Crib Shed Tearooms. The complex is open daily.

This is typical of Tasmanian towns where modern-day residents are determined to ensure that contributions of early settlers are not forgotten. Derby is one of the few places where tin is still worked, and it is also a good spot for gem fossickers.

Winnaleah — new crops

Cash cropping and dairying are important at Winnaleah, 2 km off the highway just past Derby, and visitors are welcome at the local cheese factory. In recent times this has been the setting for experimentation and subsequent export of mint, parsley and carraway seed oils. The caraway is used in the production of cosmetics, and this was the first commercial planting in Australia. Other trials are under

Miner's hut at the Derby Tin Mine Centre.

way with daisies used in pyrethrum production. The industry has a promising future in Tasmania.

The Tasman Highway continues on to Weldborough, Pyengana and St Helens, with a secondary road to Gladstone (see page 37).

Inspite of the growth of Launceston suburbs, one need not travel far on the Bass Highway before rural features begin to dominate.

Scottsdale — a business centre then and now.

Entally House — historic showpiece.

Hadspen — catering for travellers

Hadspen's Red Feather Inn probably was the first coaching station on the road from Launceston. Tearooms and a craft shop now operate in an adjoining building, and todays travellers are well catered for in hotel accommodation, a caravan and camping ground, and at Rutherglen Village.

It is hard to imagine that this holiday, convention and entertainment centre has grown in just a few years from its beginnings as a family-orientated holiday destination based on self contained cottages. Sporting interests are satisfied with tennis courts, an indoor swimming pool, canoeing and boating on the Soth Esk River, horse riding, cycling, BMX and jogging tracks. Other drawcards are an art gallery, working pottery, animal and bird sanctuary and museum. Rutherglen has a convention centre, a bar, bistro, banquet and function rooms.

Heritage preserved

Entally House, probably Tasmania's best-known historic home, is situated just west of Hadspen and is open daily (except Christmas Day). It was built in 1820 by Thomas Reibey, whose son was one of Tasmania's early Premiers. The house has antique furnishings, and the outbuildings — also from another era — include stone stables, a coach house (complete with vehicles), a bluestone chapel and a lodge.

Carrick — mill lives again

For generations an old roadside flour mill by the Liffey River has been a feature of Carrick, 17 km from Launceston, and now the previously derelict structure is breathing new life. The original mill began work in 1810, but the present bluestone mill now has a somewhat different role — as a restaurant. There's also a French restaurant and one in old stables! For goodies of another kind, Christies offers paintings, antiques and general collectables.

Carrick has a hotel and several art and craft outlets, (including one featuring copperware), and a village gallery. In recent times Carrick has developed nearly as many operations as private homes!

From Carrick a road leads off the highway to the farming township of Bracknell (hotel) and the picturesque Liffey Valley.

The heart of Tasmania

The Liffey Valley is at the geographic centre of Tasmania and often is referred to as the "heart" of the State. It is popular with bushwalkers, fishermen and day-trippers, many of whom are attracted by a fernery which has the largest range of ferns for sale in Tasmania. It is built from ti-tree and melaleuca, as are the adjacent tearooms, perched high in a wattle glade. While partaking of freshly made scones and other delights, visitors can view Drys Bluff, (the highest peak in the Great Western Tiers), and the native birdlife. The fernery is open from Wednesday to Sunday during the summer and at weekends in winter.

The Carrick mill is now a restaurant.

Threshing operations, about 1920.

Falls and forests
A short distance away Liffey Falls cascade through rainforest. It is a ¾ hour walk up to the falls if cars are parked at the base, or motorists can drive to the top of the hill and follow a short, stepped-walk to the multiple falls, a feature of the Liffey State Reserve.

Hagley — "notable connections"
St Mary's Church is the focal point at Hagley. The foundation stone was laid in 1861 by

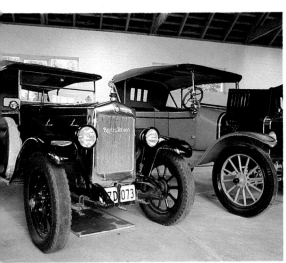
Vintage cars at the White House, Westbury.

Australia's first knight, Sir Richard Dry. The beautiful east window was one to the gifts to the church from Lady Dry.

Other attractions at Hagley are a teahouse, picnic area, and berry and flower farm.

Westbury — a store of antiques
Fitzpatrick's Inn is thought to be Westbury's first inn and opened in 1833 as the Commercial Hotel. Westbury is 34 km from Launceston and the inn is still a local landmark.

Furnishings of the colonial period are featured at the White House, but it is the 17th and 18th century oak items that prove a bonus for visitors. Built in the 1840s as Thomas White's Token Store it stands at the end of the village green (believed to be the only such green in the southern hemisphere). Outhouses shelter vintage vehicles, an extensive collection of 19th century toys, "fashions of the day", and even an early ice cream vending machine. It is managed by the National Trust.

Pearn's Steam Museum, one of the finest collections of steam engines in the southern hemisphere, and a large gemstone and minerals display should not be missed.

Another building of note in Westbury is St Andrew's Church, where there are examples of work by one of Tasmania's most famous wood-carvers, Mrs Nellie Payne, who lived in the district.

The Bass Highway continues to the farming town of Exton, where the Heidi Cheese Factory belies the town's first name, Marshy Paddock.

Devonport looking east, circa 1915.

Chocolate soils favour farming, near Ulverstone.

North West

Seaways and railways have both played a vital part in development of the North West. The region extends from Deloraine along the North West Coast to Marrawah on the West Coast, and inland to areas such as Cradle Mountain.

As settlers moved west from Launceston they made camp at successive rivers they encountered, hence the close proximity of many towns in the region today. Explorers referred to the Rubicon as the "first western river", the Mersey was the "second western river"; and so expansion continued to the Don, Forth, Leven, Blythe and Emu Rivers. Settlers soon moved along the rivers into the inland areas and began producing goods that were shipped from ports which developed in the estuaries. The railway too, was established in stages; places such as Latrobe, boomed late last century while they were the terminus for trains from Northern Tasmania.

The earliest settlements were at Stanley and Port Sorell. Stanley, in the far North West, was the headquarters of the Van Diemen's Land Company, which had been granted large areas of land for wool production, Port Sorell, was the centre from which pioneers moved west to develop Forth, then Don, Latrobe, Torquay (East Devonport) and Formby (West Devonport).

Goods exported in the early days included timber, limestone, potatoes, chaff and thousands of tons of grey peas which went to England for pigeon feed. Steel and coal for the railways were among supplies coming in by ship. The North West sometimes is referred to as a "food bowl" and it produces a significant percentage of Australia's frozen vegetables. Important secondary industries are the production of paper, timber and pelletisation of iron ore.

For more than twenty years Devonport has been Tasmania's main sea passenger terminal and Burnie is another vital cargo port. Air services link Devonport and Wynyard with Victoria and King Island, and there are daily intrastate services and light aircraft are available for scenic flights.

The overland pack track from Launceston to Circular Head was the fore-runner of today's Bass Highway. There were no bridges and rivers had to be forded. The Bass Highway links northern Tasmania with Marrawah.

Deloraine forms the first major junction as the Bass Highway heads west from Launceston.

Deloraine, a leading agricultural district.

Deloraine — classified historic town
Lush countryside surrounds Deloraine; since the 1840s it has been an important agricultural district.

Many of the town's Georgian and Victorian buildings have been restored, a number of them for commercial purposes. The Bowerbank Mill and Gallery was formerly one of Deloraine's flour mills. It now houses a first-class art and crafts display and a leather workshop. Legend has it that a gold sovereign was embedded in the tall chimney during construction. The mill is open daily except Monday. The former Family and Commercial Inn is now a museum; nowadays cider is the only brew served at the bar!

Deloraine also has antique shops, tea rooms, a full range of stores, a medical centre, hotel and motel accommodation, a caravan park, camping area and youth hostel.

Stanley — the oldest north-western town.

Still serving travellers

In the 1830s Bonney's Inn served travellers and now, after a varied "career", it is back to its original role. The coaching lunches are just as hearty as ever, and picnic hampers are also available. For those who fancy a leisurely paddle on the Meander River punts and canoes are available for hire. Details from the inn.

St Mark's Church of England, a Gothic revival building with a three-level tower and spire keeps watch over the town.

A military museum on the highway has militaria from the Boer War to modern times. Among the exhibits is a 1914 American four-wheel drive truck.

Deloraine is at the northern end of the Lake Highway which leads to the Central Highlands, and just west of the town, a road leads to Mole Creek and a number of attractions, both natural and man-made.

Lemana Junction — famous smokehouse

A small smokehouse set amid grazing country has put Lemana Junction on the map, both in Australia and overseas. It is 7 km from Deloraine on the Mole Creek Road and visitors can inspect the works by arrangement. Eels, scallops, trout and abalone are smoked or processed into items such as pates. A wide range of goods is on sale at the Smokehouse Barn.

Mole Creek — with "living" moles

At Mole Creek, 20 km west of Deloraine, a holiday village has pioneer style pine cabins with self-contained accommodation for two or four people, and next door a fairyland cave houses a unique mole village. Furry, sculpted moles go about their jobs at the bakery, gold mine, store, flour mill and around their homes. No details have been forgotten; beads are transformed into honey jars, bottle tops become pies and a "cast iron" stove looks quite unlike its original pill-bottle self. The display is open daily except Friday.

Bees buzzing round flowers could be a pointer to another attraction in the Mole Creek area — production of Tasmania's famous leatherwood honey, which can be bought from the local honey factory.

A "mole" at Mole Creek.

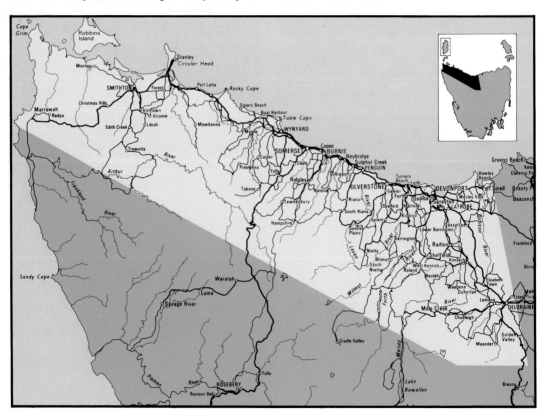

Caves and animals

There are a number of limestone caves in this area and the N.P.W.S. conducts tours through the two main ones several times daily, except Christmas Day.

King Solomon's Cave, 16 km from Mole Creek, is a dry cave with spacious passageways in one large cavern — good for people who do not like that ''closed-in'' feeling. Marakoopa Cave, 11 km from Mole Creek, has two underground streams, glowworms and gypsum formations. It was discovered in 1910 during a search for lost cattle.

Animals of other kinds — including wallabies, wombats and kangaroos — can be seen in a free-range wildlife park, and a nocturnal house contains Tasmanian devils, native cats, sugar gliders, possums and other Tasmanian species. The snakes are not free-ranging — they are enclosed! There are picnic and barbecue areas at the park ...

Back on the Bass Highway, Elizabeth Town (10 km west of Deloraine) has a showroom filled with blackwood furniture as well as crafts and souvenirs. Potatoes grown in the rich chocolate soils of the North West are among produce for sale along the roadside, and raspberry lovers should not miss the Christmas Hills Raspberry Farm between December and May.

Latrobe — "home" of cycling

First settled in the late 1830s, Latrobe rose to prominence when it was the terminus for trains during construction of the north-western railway line 40 years later. It has always been the shopping centre for surrounding rural areas, but during its heyday it was also the base for a brewery and cider factory (using apples from nearby Spreyton), and for extraction of oil from large shale deposits in the district. This process stopped more than 50 years ago, but old-timers still remember the unforgettable odour it produced!

In the 1930s the Latrobe main store would buy the local blackberries — and it was quite a massive exercise. Bevan Wells, the third of four generations of his family which has run the store since 1893, remembered the annual ''operation''.

Thousands of acres of blackberries grew along roadsides, rivers and creeks. Sheep and goats nibbled them, but income derived from blackberry gathering also paid for winter clothes for many children. Often the storekeeper would give clothing to the value of blackberries he bought from the pickers; the items had to be purchased before the end of April.

Five hundred blackberry casks were kept at the store until the end of February, when they were brought out, filled with water, and had hoops tightened down. Bevan often joined his father on a motor lorry as he travelled round the district to places such as Spreyton, Aberdeen, Beulah and Sheffield. Pickers would bring their blackberries to the side of the truck, where they were weighed and purchased for one farthing per 1½ pounds.

On the return to Latrobe the blackberries were packed in different sized casks. The next stage involved railing them to Devonport, from where they were shipped to Melbourne. Bevan's father accompanied the cargo to Victoria, and if there was no market for it at Melbourne's jam factory he sometimes had to travel as far as Shepparton to find a buyer. The outbreak of World War II put an end to the blackberry buying; however, a record crop of 160 tons was picked in 1939.

There was a ready market for goods of all sorts and Bevan remembered the planning and organisation that went into visits by commercial travellers. Hotels had sample rooms reserved for travellers, who spent up to one day unpacking their wares from huge wicker baskets. Merchants called by appointment, and items ordered arrived about two weeks later — often quicker than today!

Bell's Parade at Latrobe used to be lined with warehouses handling goods from the railway as well as cargo from small ketches and barges which came up the Mersey inlet. Now it is lined with extensive picnic, barbecue and recreation areas.

Bell's Parade, Latrobe.

There was time to relax too, in the ''olden days''. More than 3,000 people attended the first carnival conducted by the United Australian Axemen's Association in 1891, and the previous year a cycling club had been formed in Latrobe. This later became known as the Bicycle Race Club. Today one of Australia's biggest cycling carnivals, the Latrobe Wheel Race, is held each Christmas.

Museum — no offenders now

Hundreds of people passed through the Latrobe courts many of them charged with sheep and cattle stealing, but visitors now come for more pleasant purposes. The court is no longer in session, but some exhibits on display still provide a useful record ... They are in a museum which is open on Friday and Sunday afternoons, and the dock, witness stand and magistrate's bench are all still in place.

The Devon Cottage Hospital, established in 1889, was the first hospital on the North West

Coast. Later it was replaced with the Devon Hospital and the current establishment, the Mersey General Hospital and training school.

Port Sorell — oldest N.W. town
During early days of settlement this port, 19 km east of Devonport, was visited by sealers and fishermen, and was known as the "First Western River". In 1805 a report from Lieutenant Symons of the **Integrity**, stated that "the country between the Supply River and York Town had been found so good it was intended to give the first free settlers locations of land in that district". An industry which helped develop the port was collection and stripping of wattle bark along the Rubicon River and Green's Creek.

Like many small towns Port Sorell (originally named Burgess) has experienced changing fortunes. It declined in importance and population as Devonport grew, but now its mild climate is encouraging visitors, and they are catered for in diverse ways. The Shearwater Country Club has tennis, golf, bicycle hire, swimming and indoor games facilities, motel accommodation and a licensed restaurant. Port Sorell also has a caravan park, camping area and holiday cottages. There are a number of shops and one, in Squeaking Point Road, specialises in Welsh tweeds and tapestries. At Freers Beach surf cats, canoes, sailboards and boats are available for hire at weekends and public holidays between October and March. It is a good area for walking and all forms of aquatic activities. Nearby Hawley Beach also has sailcraft hire.

Asbestos Range National Park — horse riding
East of Port Sorell the Asbestos Range National Park extends to Greens Beach over more than 4,000 ha of beach and dune country. People with their own horses can use trails from the ranger's house at the western end of the park, which has two camping sites. Mineral asbestos was mined here late last century.

The road from Port Sorell to Devonport passes timber operations at Wesley Vale and the Devonport Airport, one of the two major air outlets in the North West.

Devonport — Gateway to Tasmania
In 1890 the towns of Formby and Torquay joined to become Devonport and it is now one of the State's five cities, with a population of more than 23,000.

Many of the area's early buildings were destroyed by fire, but there remains plenty of evidence of development. (In 1896 it was made an offence to allow cattle to wander the main streets of East Devonport!)

Devonport became a vital port and the Bluff Lighthouse built in 1889 is still a landmark. The light is visible up to 27 km out to sea. The Bluff, itself, has sheltered beaches, good picnic and recreation areas, rock fishing, and a caravan park.

All types of accommodation, stores and sporting facilities are available in Devonport, and there are both unlicensed and licensed restaurants (including old world Ruby's), convention areas and a Tasmanian Travel Centre in Rooke Street.

Coastal view near Devonport.

In recent times Devonport owes much of its progress to its siting as the Tasmanian terminal for the passenger/cargo ferry service from Victoria. It is also a base for vehicle hire, including campervans and holiday homes. For more than 100 years locally produced goods have been shipped out of the port, but recently textiles, carpets, meat and vegetables have become important exports.

For a short trip a ferry makes regular crossings of the Mersey.

Tiagarra — aboriginal displays
Rock carvings found in this area in 1929 give an insight into the lifestyle of the Tasmanian Aborgines, and it is possible to learn about this ancient race from displays at Tiagarra (an Aboriginal word for keep), a culture and art centre at the Bluff headland. The centre is open daily.

Aboriginal displays at Tiagarra.

Transport of all kinds

The Don River Railway, on the western outskirts of the city, has a full-sized passenger train in operation, and a steam railway museum contains restored locomotives. By contrast, the Tasmanian Maritime and Folk Museum has detailed models from the days of sail, while pedal boats and aqua bikes are among vehicles for hire. In addition, a ferry makes regular crossings of the river.

Taswegia combines an historic Print Museum, graphic design centre and craft gallery. Impressions, in the Devonport Showcase, where there is a full range of tourist information, specialises in Tasmanian timber products. The Wilderness Shop in Stewart Street has keepsakes and details on activities in the State.

Serendipity is a waterside wonderland, where bumper boats, dodgem cars, canoes, the Martin Cash bushranger shootout and a host of other attractions provide thrills and spills.

Home Hill, in Middle Road, once the home of former Prime Minister Joseph Lyons and Dame Enid Lyons, Australia's first woman member of Cabinet, is open several afternoons each week. Details from the Tasmanian Travel Centre.

Apples are still an important crop in the Mersey Valley, especially in the Spreyton district (another early settlement which had its own cider factory). Mushrooms are grown here, too. A pleasant round trip from Devonport passes through Spreyton, Railton, Sheffield and back via Lower Barrington.

Devonport is also a base for trips to Gowrie Park and the Cradle Mountain-Lake St Clair National Park. A number of escorted, fully equipped tours operate to the Cradle Valley or Lake St Clair (details from Tasmanian Travel Centres). There are light aircraft charter flights, and hiking clubs organise walking trips.

Railton — cement works

One of Tasmania's main industries — the Goliath Portland Cement Company — is based at Railton, 23 km from Devonport, an on-site quarry providing raw materials. Railton has a hotel and camping area.

Sheffield — picturesque setting

Standing at the foothills of the Great Western Tiers and the majestic Mt Roland (1,234 m), Sheffield has developed into a living art gallery as a result of its huge outdoor murals depicting subjects of local interest. The Blacksmith Gallery is worth a visit, and the Lake Barrington and Mersey-Forth hydro developments are just 10 km away.

Gowrie park — modern-day pioneers

The arts of horse-shoeing, whip-plaiting, broom-making and shingle-splitting have not been lost. At Gowrie Park, 41 km from Devonport, they are taught to visitors staying at the Black Stumps Pioneer Settlement, where a working bullock team also displays its prowess. Dormitory accommodation is available (plus a cook, if required), but advance bookings are essential. Gowrie Park is the administration and workshop headquarters for the Mersey-Forth power scheme.

Rowing at Lake Barrington.

Cradle Mountain-Lake St Clair National Park

This national park is one of the most glaciated areas in Australia, with mountain peaks, alpine moorlands, lakes, tarns and a wide range of flora and fauna.

Cradle Mountain (1,546 m) and Barn Bluff dominate the northern section of the 126,000 ha park, and an 85 km overland track runs through to Lake St Clair at the southern end. In the centre of the park a track leads to Tasmania's highest mountain, Mt Ossa (1,617 m).

Weather changes abruptly, and the park has claimed a number of lives. Walkers should

Cradle Mountain is a photographer's paradise.

ensure they have adequate equipment and provisions. N.P.W.S. rangers are stationed at both ends of the park, and there is a small entry charge. The Cradle Mountain Lodge and Waldheim Chalet are just over 80 km from Devonport. The last section of the road is unsealed and ends at Dove Lake. Sights en route include Post Office Tree. The early settlers, whose activities ranged from timber cutting to butter making, used to leave and collect their mail from this particular tree.

In addition to lodge accommodation there are self-contained cabins and a new campground, where buildings blend with the environment. Recreation and convention facilities are available at the Lodge. Meals and petrol can be obtained from the Lodge, which has a licensed restaurant, but there is no store for general supplies. Tame wallabies and possums make the most of any leftovers!

This area is ideal for bushwalking, birdwatching, climbing and photography.

Waldheim — a dream come true

In 1912 Gustav Weindorfer, regarded as the founder of this park, built a chalet from King Billy pine. It has recently been restored and fitted out with bunks. Accommodation also is available in huts, but all must be booked in advance with the N.P.W.S. which will answer any queries about walking or staying in the Cradle Mountain-Lake St Clair National Park.

Magnificent as it is, this is not an area where any risks should be taken ...

After leaving Devonport, the Bass Highway

follows the north west coastline of Tasmania —surely one of the world's most beautiful highway journeys.

Turner's Beach is a holiday resort mid-way between Devonport and Ulverstone, where there are holiday flats, a camping area and caravan parks, including one with private facilities. The beach is near the Forth River (good for mullet and salmon fishing) and a short distance away is Forth (originally named Hamilton-on-Forth), the second settlement in this part of Tasmania. The township has hotel accommodation.

Ulverstone war memorial.

Ulverstone — fine beaches

The hub of a rich farming and tourist district, Ulverstone (122 km from Launceston) is situated on the Leven River and originally was called "The Leven". Fishing is good in the river and estuary. By river it is possible to reach two barbecue and picnic spots developed on the river bank, and stops can be made for passengers to wander in the fern glades.

Australia's largest quick-frozen vegetable processors, Edgell Birdseye, a division of Petersville Industries Limited, has a factory in Ulverstone. Timber, furniture and masonry industries are also important.

Ulverstone has a full range of accommodation (including well-appointed caravan parks), shopping and sporting facilities. Crafts on sale include hand-made copperware, the maker of which can be seen at Weeda in Forth Road. A feature of the town centre is a shrine of remembrance to people who served in World War II.

Timber — for various purposes

Timber was an important product for 19th century settlers, who quickly replaced their tents and bark huts with cottages made from slab and palings. They had shingle roofs and often were lined only with pages from magazines. The shingle and paling splitters have gone, but there is one activity involving timber which is still flourishing — the sport of competitive woodchopping. This began in Ulverstone in 1870, blocks being much larger in those days ...

Leven Canyon — dramatic

The Leven Canyon is a spectacular gorge 36 km south of Ulverstone. It is reached via Sprent, Castra and Nietta (where Kaydale Lodge host farm has accommodation for seven people) and this journey also has many outstanding views.

There are numerous walking tracks at the Canyon — one from picnic grounds leads to a lookout that is actually over the canyon; a memorable sight, but not one for the faint-hearted! The Jean Brook Waterfall is reached via a lower cliff walk.

Gunns Plains — hops and caves

There are glowworms and a freshwater stream in the limestone caves at Gunns Plains, 23 km from Ulverstone. Tours of the illuminatd caves last 40 minutes and begin on the hour daily between 10 a.m. and 4 p.m. (There are steep steps at the entrance.)

Hops are produced in the area and many are exported. Fields can be seen from the road and harvesting occurs in mid March. The drying kiln here is one of the largest and most technically advanced in the world.

Pleasant picnic spots include one at Victoria Park.

It is worth diverting off the Bass Highway between Ulverstone and Penguin, and following a scenic route along the coast. Features include the Three Sisters, off-shore rock formations which form part of a seabird sanctuary.

Penguins — real and unreal

Penguin is a residential rather than an industrial township. First settled in 1861, it took its name from the fairy penguins still found in rookeries along the coast. Early activities centred on timber, with palings being sent from here for use in Melbourne buildings.

The town centre is dominated by a fibro-cement penguin on the foreshore which commemorates the centenary of the proclamation of the town, and even the nearby rubbish bins are in the shape of penguins! There are nightly tours of the penguin rookery between November and March, from the Penguin Caravan Park.

Penguin caters well for sport and recreation. There is a sports centre in Ironcliffe Road and the Dial Range Sports and Recreation Complex between Mt Montgomery and the Bass Highway has facilities for bowling, pony trails, golf, tennis, motorcycle scrambling, mini-bike riding and hockey.

Magnificent views can be obtained from lookouts in the Dial Range State Forest which adjoins the sports area. Walking tracks have been cut by the Forestry Commission and the N.P.W.S.

Burnie — busy port

The first residents of Burnie (originally named Emu Bay because of the large numbers of these birds in the area) were a blacksmith, carpenter, sawyer and farming servant. That was back in the 1820s, but by the turn of the century, Burnie (named after Van Diemen's Land Company director William Burnie) had a population of 1,000, largely as a result of the

Leven Canyon — a spectacular gorge.

boom which accompanied discovery of tin at Waratah's Mt Bischoff. Bagged tin ore, timber and farm produce were shipped out of Burnie. It is still an important port ... and now has more than 20,000 residents in the municipality. Facilities have improved considerably since the 1870s when passengers came close to shore in rowboats, then climbed into a basket to be hauled aloft by a crane!

Modern exports include timber, dairy products, minerals, paper products and vegetables. Multi-million dollar developments stand where Chinese market gardeners once grew vegetables for Burnie and West Coast mining towns.

Burnie, a vital port of long standing.

Paper plays a part

Burnie is the centre of the paper industry, and the Associated Pulp and Paper Mills Ltd is the largest employer in the city. The plant can be inspected Monday to Thursday at 2 p.m. but bookings are essential and children under 10 are not admitted. Much of the paper is shipped from the port, which is the terminal for Australian National Line "Searoad" cargo vessels.

Other industries include Tioxide Australia Pty Ltd (which produces titanium products), Lactos Pty Ltd (where visitors can arrange to view manufacture of continental style cheeses), and Tasmanian Plywood Mills. There are large interstate and overseas markets for local timber — eucalypts, sassafras, myrtle, blackwood and celery top pine. Milk from the North West is used in butter production and in the manufacture of chocolate in Hobart.

Railway replaces bullocks

Initially bullock drays were used to bring minerals to Burnie, then a horse drawn tramway took over, and finally a steel railway was built by the Emu Bay and Mt Bischoff Railway Co. Now the Emu Bay Railway is the only privately owned railway system in Tasmania.

Early history is featured in the Loco Bar of the Burnie Town House, while there is memorabilia of many kinds at the Pioneer Village Museum in High Street.

Potions, hat pins and phonographs

We travel back in time in the museum which recreates Burnie's commercial centre between 1890 and 1910; Bell's Livery Stable, Edward Evans' Boot Shop, a coffee palace, blacksmithing and wheelwright operations, a dental surgery, and the inevitable inn. The technology room, with its cottage piano, wireless sets, box cameras and old sewing machines, illustrates the progress in the past 100 years. The museum is open during the day, Monday to Friday, and in the afternoon at weekends (closed Christmas and Anzac Day, and Good Friday).

Crafts and conventions

Burnie has numerous art and craft outlets and galleries, items for sale including goods made by leatherworkers and spinning and weaving enthusiasts. Osborne House and the Art Gallery in Wilmot Street are worth a visit, and Burnie's Civic Centre is the focal point for entertainment and cultural activities. Tasmanian timbers have been used extensively in the foyer, theatres and reception rooms. Conventions are held in the Town Hall, which can seat 1,000 people.

Inn and emus

Burnie Park has attractions to suit all ages. In its restful grounds is a section for animals and birds including wallabies, ducks, peacocks and those "orginal settlers" — emus. Children can clamber over an old steam loco. The reconstructed Burnie Inn is the city's oldest building; it was first licensed in 1847 and operated till 1900. The park also has tennis courts and a music bowl.

Burnie has all types of accommodation, vehicle hire, shops and both unlicensed and licensed restaurants.

Just a drive away

A short distance from Burnie there are the Guide Falls (17 km south on the road to West Ridgley), a pine plantation with picnic and barbecue areas (5 km south of Upper Natone), and Fern Glade (a short distance from the highway along Old Surrey Road) — an ideal sport for picnicking or walking among trees and ferns.

Somerset — satellite town

The Waratah Highway from the West Coast joins the Bass Highway at Somerset, 6 km from Burnie. The main industries here are the bulk frozen food operations (open to the public), timber and plywood mills and industrial machinery. Inland from Somerset are the dairying districts of Elliott and Yolla, and the beautiful Hellyer Gorge. At Parrawe there are experi-

Pioneer Village Museum, Burnie.

Burnie Inn.

mental re-plantings of eucalyptus and pine trees. The original trees of the rainforest were ring-barked and left to die during land clearing operations after World War I.

Hellyer Gorge — reserve
The serene forests and attractive grounds make the Hellyer Gorge an appealing rest area, 40 km south of Somerset. There are shelters, toilets and barbecues in the reserve on the banks of the Hellyer River, and identification of many trees adds to interest along well-formed tracks.

Yolla — milk churns tell all
If you are in any doubt about what sort of area this is, then simply take a look at some of the mail "boxes" ... They're milk churns. "We're thankful for every tankful", says the sign on a Yolla petrol station, and it is a slogan that reflects moves to rationalise numbers of outlets in Tasmania. Handcrafted goods are made and sold at Which ? Craft Village in the Old Yolla Butter Factory.

Yolla is 23 km from Burnie and a secondary highway, via Mt Hicks, leads to Wynyard.

Wynyard — planes and fishing boats
Wynyard combines the qualities of a township serving cash crop and dairying industries with those of a fishing port. The town is on the Inglis River, 16 km from Burnie, and there are extensive picnic, barbecue and recreation areas along the foreshore at the Gutteridge Gardens.

Wynyard has one of the two airports on the North West Coast (the other is at Devonport). As well as interstate and King Island flights by major carriers, light aircraft operators offer short scenic flights or trips farther afield to places such as western, south-western and highland areas, in single or twin-engine planes.

One of the main industries is the Table Cape Cheese Factory (where a cheese bar has mild, mature and vintage cheeses on sale) and the factory can be inspected from September to May, or by appointment each Thursday. Other industries include sawmills and the Tasmanian Plywood Mills. Butter, milk powder and meat are produced in this rich dairying district and the United Milk Tasmania Company in Goldie Street is an important processor.

On the accommodation scene there are villas, budget units or vans at the extensive Leisure Ville complex in East Wynyard, hotels, motels, caravan, camping and youth hostel facilities, and country accommodation. Crafts worth watching out for include pictures and jewellery made from bark of native melaleucas.

Fishing and fossils
The search for trout leads anglers to the Inglis and Flowerdale Rivers and the waterways are also good for power boating, yachting and water skiing. A scuba centre at East Wynyard has equipment for hire, and an instructor.

At Fossil Bluff (beyond the golf course) the world's oldest fossil marsupial was found at the face of the Bluff when rock was being removed for use in a breakwater at the mouth of the Inglis River. The Bluff's soft sandstone has many fossils of shells deposited when the level of Bass Strait was much higher.

Table Cape — lighthouse
At Table Cape steps lead down to a vantage point for viewing the superb scenic coastline. The lookout is equipped with binoculars. However, only those with a head for heights should descend as there is a sheer drop to the rocky shore below. (There is a fence, though!)

Table Cape, named by Bass and Flinders in 1798, has been a landmark for travellers for centuries, and the Table Cape Lighthouse still guides "men of the sea". It can be reached by a secondary road which follows the coast beyond Wynyard and re-joins the Bass Highway near Boat Harbour.

The "dog bone" at Oldina Forest Reserve.

Oldina Forest Reserve — "dog bone"
The entrance to the Oldina Forest Reserve, 7 km south of Wynyard, features a "dog bone", an ancient Huon pine log used in a boom across the Pieman River. The boom was constructed to collect logs that had been felled upstream and swept down by periodic floods. Native trees blend with pines introduced as far back as 1920. Willows, Douglas firs and poplars add their grandeur to the reserve which has extensive picnic and playground areas. The surrounding forest is used for pony trekking (and horses and ponies can be hired at Pine Lodge, on Deep Creek Road just south of Wynyard), trail-bike riding, fishing and bush-walking.

Boat Harbour Beach — clear waters
The small rural township of Boat Harbour is on the Bass Highway, 14 km west of Wynyard, and just past the town a road leads 3 km off the highway to Boat Harbour Beach. A sheltered resort, it is noted for its rock and coral formations and clear waters; ideal for underwater pursuits, swimming and fishing. At low tide it is sometimes possible to see abalone on the rocks. Basalt soil extends right to the beach to provide a striking contrast of green slopes and blue waters.

A BYO restaurant specialises in seafoods and visitors have a choice of two motels, including the Seaway Motel, with its own hydrotherapeutic and leisure centre, indoor heated pool, spa and sauna, plus a licensed restaurant and seminar room. Cottages, flats, overnight cabins and a caravan park complete the range of accommodation facilities.

Sisters Beach — special Banksia
A short distance away in the Rocky Cape National Park, is Sisters Beach. Here there is the possibility of a rare sight — the eyrie of the sea eagle. Birdland native gardens and a nursery are open daily, and visitors also can see a superb collection of photographs and other specimens of birds, animals and orchids of the district.

Well marked nature trails reveal delights such as Banksia Serrata, a gnarled, rugged tree found only at Sisters Beach. Sometimes known as Saw Banksia because of its serrated leaves, the bushes, with their large yellow brush flowers, were apparently isolated in this small pocket when Tasmania was cut off from the mainland. The best viewing time is February, but any time is good for viewing some of the 60 species of birds identified in the area. They are attracted by native plants, shrubs and trees. Plants, ferns and craftwork (including local timber products) are on sale and there is limited accommodation in small bush cottages.

Massive rhododendrons
Some of the rhododendrons at Lapoinya Gardens are more than six metres high. They are set in rainforest, 5 km south of Sisters Creek, which is west of Boat Harbour on the Bass Highway. Soon after turning into Scotts Road

A firetail at Sisters Beach.

signposts direct visitors to the gardens. Late October, summer and autumn offer the most dramatic displays and liliums and naturalised fuschias add to the spectacle. There are also numerous forest walking tracks.

Rocky Cape National Park — heath
Geological features, coastal heath vegetation and birdlife (including parrots and honey eaters) are the main points of interest in the Rocky Cape National Park, 31 km west of Wynyard. This was a favourite hunting ground of Tasmanian Aborigines and evidence of their occupation has been found in a number of caves and middens. The park has numerous walking tracks, and it is a good area for shell collectors, fishing enthusiasts and photographers.

Shell collecting near Rocky Cape National Park.

Rocky Cape — historic links
Counter meals are available from Tuesday to Sunday and there are barbecue facilities at a tavern west of Rocky Cape. The Cape was named by Matthew Flinders in 1798. Nowadays the necessities of life are stocked in the former school house! Timber from the district used to be milled near the Detention River, where pleasant picnic spots include Myoora Park, developed by Rural Youth Club members.

Port Latta — man-made masterpiece
Huge bulk ore carriers from Japan load pelletised iron ore at Port Latta. This man-made port is between Rocky Cape and Stanley at the end of an 85 km pipeline which carries crushed ore in slurry form from mines at Savage River. Tours of the plant start at 2 p.m. each Friday, but children under 12 are not allowed. Flat shoes and trousers should be worn. Last century boats called at flimsy wooden jetties and even beaches along this coast, and it is unlikely that traders of those days could even imagine what massive developments would take place in the 1960s.

Dip Falls — honey, too
At Black River, 5 km west of Port Latta, a road leads to Dip Falls. Forests near here contain a number of giant eucalypts. Leatherwood and clover honey — as well as the unusual black-berry honey — are produced here. There are picnic spots at the falls, but watch out for log trucks on the winding road.

Stanley — port and famous citizen
Ships have been calling at Stanley since 1826. Whalers were among the early visitors and later freighters used it as a base for carrying goods to and from the Victorian goldfields.

Crayfish is one of the seafoods now handled at the deep water port, and it is possible to inspect the fish processing plant at the wharf. Stanley is a classified historic town, and restored buildings include a small timber cottage which, in 1879, was the birthplace of Joseph Lyons, the only Tasmanian to become an Australian Prime Minister.

The Van Diemen's Land Company made its headquarters in Stanley in 1826, and Bi-centennial funding has facilitated some rest-oration of Highfield, home of the Company's chief agent. The property includes stables, stockyards and general outbuildings.

The Nut — like "a cake"
There are expansive views from The Nut, which Bass and Flinders said resembled a Christmas cake! The 120m high summit of this basalt formation can be reached by chairlift or via a walking track. Galleon Tearooms are strategically located for refreshments!

It is believed that the well known colonial architect John Lee Archer, a magistrate in Stanley, died at Poet's Cottage, once a school for ladies and gentlemen. Along with surveyor Henry Hellyer, he is buried in the old cemetery at the foot of The Nut.

The Nut is a Stanley landmark.

History inside and out
Period furnishings, household items, pioneering relics, photographs, minerals and gemstones are among items on display in the Discovery Centre. There is also an outstanding collection of shell work.

The Plough Inn, built in 1843, has had a varied "career", serving for a period as a dispensary, and now as a private home. It is open for inspection.

Another of the early inns, now called the Union Motel, still provides accommodation. A feature of the hotel is the magnificent stone-arched cellar. Stanley also has a caravan and camping area with kitchen, laundry and barbecue facilities. Gull Cottage, overlooking Godfreys Beach, is open daily (except Tuesdays) for lunches and Devonshire teas.

A highlight of the year is the Circular Head Arts Festival each September.

Van Diemen's Land Company building at Stanley.

The Plough Inn at Stanley.

Smithton — timber and timber goods

Blackwood is one of Tasmania's finest furniture timbers, and three quarters of the annual cut comes from the Circular Head district. The species is a member of the wattle family and grows 20 to 30 metres tall.

A number of Smithton industries are based on timber production. Kauri Timber is the largest hardwood sawmill in the southern hemisphere. Visitors can view milling and drying operations at 2 p.m., by appointment, but children under 12 are not allowed. By arrangement, it is possible to see furniture and woodwork production by Britton Brothers in Mill Road, and souvenirs made from local blackwood, myrtle, sassafras, leatherwood and celery top pine are available in King Street. Plywood, paper, pulp and woodchips are important by-products of the sawmills.

Premier primary products

Butter and cheese are among Smithton's important primary products. Arrangements can be made to view operations at United Milk Tasmania Ltd which processes milk powder and meat. This is the headquarters of General Jones' Ltd vegetable processing section, which produces Australia's largest variety of frozen vegetables. Lacrum Commercial Research Dairy Farm is open each afternoon, while the humble spud takes on a new dimension at a recently opened multi-million dollar potato processing plant.

For inspections of a different kind there are dolomite mining works one km from the town centre. The dolomite (magnesium limestone) is used for agricultural purposes and this is the largest deposit in the Commonwealth.

Smithton has hotel-motel, caravan and camping facilities, and it is popular for boating (especially power boating), fishing and other aquatic activities.

Milk — or manferns!

There are excellent views from Tier Hill and scenic drives from Smithton include ones to Edith Creek (16 km to the south), where visitors can inspect a milk condensing plant, and to the Milkshakes Forest Reserve near the Arthur River (45 km south of Smithton). Massive manferns, myrtles, fungi and lichen are found in the reserve, which has rustic shelters, barbecues and firewood. Montagu, 16 km west of Smithton, is ideal for picnics, swimming and fishing.

Woolnorth — past and present

A 22,000 ha property on the north west tip of Tasmania is the only remaining holding of the Van Diemen's Land Company, which was responsible for the early development of the region. Situated 47 km west of Smithton, it is open for escorted bus tours from Burnie or Smithton on Mondays from January to May, with additional trips each Wednesday in January and February (details from Tasmanian Travel Centres, which also have information on four-wheel drive trips by Farnor' West Tours. These include north-western and west coast adventure expeditions, with an escape to Robbins Island providing the ultimate in

'alternative' holidays). At Woolnorth, shearers, working stock horses and sheep dogs are seen in action. There is a chance to visit Cape Grim, site of the Commonwealth Base Line Air Pollution Station, and view remains of the **Colloboi**, wrecked in 1932 at Woolnorth Point.

Marrawah — "end of the line"

From Smithton the Bass Highway leads 48 km to Marrawah, the last town on the sealed road, and one of the State's most western points.

At nearby Green Point there are picnic grounds with barbecues and toilet facilities, and a camping ground.

Aboriginal carvings from Mount Cameron West.

At Mt Cameron West near Green Point, there is a series of 50 Tasmanian Aboriginal rock carvings, regarded as the greatest surviving example of this form of art. The circles and bird tracks resemble carvings found in desert areas of mainland Australia. They are not accessible to the general public but copies of the work are displayed at the Tasmanian Museum and Art Gallery in Hobart and the Zeehan Mining Museum. West Point, to the south, has been declared a reserve so that relics and the environment are protected. Another important site for Aboriginal studies is Hunter Island, 6 km off the North West Coast.

Arthur River — adventure land

A mainly sealed road leads 15 km south from Marrawah to the Arthur River, now traversed by a single track bridge which enables further penetration of this rugged area — mainly by off-road vehicles. Temma, a base for professional fishermen and a small kelp harvesting industry, and the old mining town of Balfour are farther south.

The cruiser **George Robinson** travels upstream to the junction with the Frankland River several times each week.

An alternative return route to Smithton goes south from Marrawah, inland near Rebecca Creek, and on forestry roads via Edith Creek. There are no shops or petrol supplies between Marrawah and Edith Creek on this road.

King and Flinders Islands

Tasmanians often consider themselves isolated and "left off the map", but probably none so much as the residents of the State's two main off-shore islands, King and Flinders, which guard the western and eastern entrances to Bass Strait. While it may have led to some commercial disadvantages over the years, their isolation has proved an advantage to todays travellers who find them havens of peace and tranquility.

KING ISLAND
Captain Reid in the schooner **Martha** discovered King Island at the western end of Bass Strait in 1798, and in 1801 it was named in honour of Governor King of New South Wales. Today the island's main links are with Tasmania and Victoria.

The 126,000 ha island is one of the world's main producers of scheelite, used in the manufacture of armaments. Mining has been important since the early 1900s. Industries such as kelp drying now have replaced the sealing activities that were important in the early 19th century.

The stormy seas of Bass Strait have claimed many victims over the years. At least 57 ships have been wrecked on King Island's coast which now provides a fascinating area for skin divers to explore.

A roll-on/roll-off cargo vessel operates between Stanley, King Island and Melbourne. Several airlines run services to and from Launceston, Hobart, Wynyard and Melbourne.

Currie — administration
Currie, on the west coast, is the administration centre. It has a motel, caravan park, units, licensed restaurant, hospital, and hire cars, with recreational facilities for golf, tennis, bowls, hockey, netball.

Grassy — port
The south east town of Grassy is almost entirely owned by King Island Scheelite Ltd. Its deep-water port is the main one for the island, and the township has tennis, badminton, golf and basketball facilities, shops and a licensed club.

Naracoopa — fuel source
A floating pipeline carries fuel from tankers to bulk storage tanks at Naracoopa, and supplies are distributed from here to all the island's industries and services. Holiday units are available at Naracoopa, once a second port for cargo vessels.

Fishing (especially cray and abalone), cheese-making, abbatoir and livestock industries are important, but, from a visitors' point of

King Island Dairy products.

view, the island's main attractions are its scenery, rich wildlife (including pheasant, rare platypus, ducks and quail), fishing (from rocks, beaches and lakes), and other aquatic activities at beaches and lagoons. The Lavinia Nature Reserve on the north east coast is an important breeding refuge for waterbirds.

King Island Dairy brie and cheddar cheeses, cultured cream and butter have achieved national recognition as gourmet products. The Dairy is open on weekdays and Saturday morning for tastings and sales.

FLINDERS ISLAND
For generations Flinders Island at the eastern end of Bass Strait has lured visitors. Some have been temporary — sailors, sealers and prospectors — but others have stayed to settle on this fascinating land in the Furneaux group of islands off Tasmania's north east tip. Many people had no choice about their destination. Flinders Island has many shipwrecks along is shores, some of them still visible, and this was where the last full-blooded Tasmanian Aboriginals were sent in the 1830s.

Aboriginal legacy
The Aborigines never adapted to life on the island and, when numbers continued to decline, the remaining few were taken on their last long journey — to Oyster Cove in southern Tasmania.

On Flinders Island they were based at what is now known as Settlement Point. The Aboriginals called it Wybalenna (blackmans houses), and its historic significance is commemorated in the brick chapel, now restored

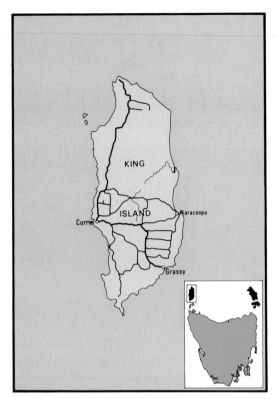

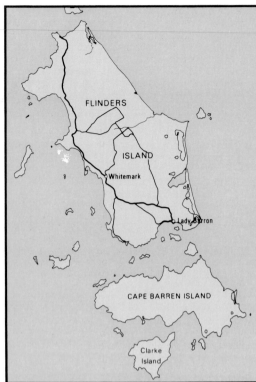

by the National Trust. This is the only building in existence which was associated with Tasmania's Aborigines. The poignant inscriptions in the cemetery at Settlement Point tell a sad story, but the Aboriginal blood lines and heritage are carried today by many islanders, especially on Cape Barren Island.

Associations with the sea
Flinders Island still retains its strong links with the sea. It was named after navigator Matthew Flinders who first charted the area, and although men no longer hunt seals, sea lions and sea elephants on the rocky outcrops, they reap rich harvests from the sea in the form of scale-fish, scallops, abalone and crayfish.

Lady Barron at the southern end of the island is the main fishing centre and is also a port for shipping livestock. It has an excellent tavern with motel accommodation, a licensed restaurant and counter meals. Holiday cottages can be hired in the area.

A lookout near Lady Barron has views to the wreck of the **Farsund** and across to Cape Barren Island. This is the only other Furneaux island with permanent habitation. It has a landing strip and wharf, and fishing is the main industry.

Water and sky for entry
The main means of entry to Flinders Island today is by air and Pats River, 5 km from the main centre of Whitemark, is one of Australia's busiest provincial airports. There are also services into Lady Barron.

Whitemark is the commercial and administrative "capital". There is accommodation in units en route from the airport, while the town itself has hotels (including the Interstate which still serves hearty, old-fashioned meals), a guest house, holiday cottages, and a number of farms in nearby areas which open their doors to visitors. Among these is a host farm at Emita which caters for five people. Whitemark has cars, campervans, caravans and motor bikes for hire. The **Strait Lady** fishing charter vessel operates from Lady Barron or Whitemark.

A changing scene
Flinders Island is a land of contrasts. Granite peaks such as Mt Strzelecki are ideal for photographers and artists. But they were not as fruitful for prospectors who searched for the source of samples of gold and tin shown to them by the Aborigines. The island has many sandy beaches some of which stretch as far as the eye can see.

Cape Barren geese.

Unique wildlife

Cape Barren geese and mutton birds are "notables" among the island's birdlife which also includes quail, ducks, pelicans and swans. At one stage numbers of the grey Cape Barren geese declined and it was feared they would become extinct. However, their numbers are now increasing and they are a feature at various locations — some as far away as Maria Island.

Flinders sometimes has been called the Island of Moonbirds. "Youla" was an Aboriginal word for moonbirds, referred to nowadays as mutton birds.

An amazing exercise

Mutton-birding is a source of income for many Furneaux islanders but it also marks a stage of the remarkable life cycle of the Youla. The birds arrive from the northern hemisphere in September and clean out their burrows of the previous year. They then leave for a short while before returning in November for the breeding period, which lasts until mid April. Baby birds are left to fend for themselves and it is at this stage that the "birders" move in. During the next few weeks hunters gather thousands of chicks for local and overseas markets, while the survivors continue to thrive and prepare for their first big flight.

Museum has the records

There are many places of interest on the 75 km road between Lady Barron and Palana at the northern tip, and the 33 km section from White-mark across to Memana and on to the soldier settlements and lagoons on the east coast.

Items salvaged from shipwrecks, early records, and some superb shells are among items displayed at a museum established by the Historical Research Association at Emita, near Settlement Point. It is appropriately housed

A mutton bird on Flinders Island.

in a building which was the first government subsidised school on the island.

"Diamonds" forever

One of the most serenic places is Killiecrankie Bay in the north west of the Island. Shell and driftwood collectors roam the dunes and a wrecked boat provides tangible evidence that these are not always friendly shores. The area is also the source of the famous Killiecrankie diamonds. Many people have been fooled into thinking these white topaze are true diamonds. A local resident uses a dredge to recover the white topaze (along with the many types of gemstones found in the area) and if you don't make a find of your own he may be able to help out!

Flinders Island is a paradise for fishermen, for people who want to believe the world is their own as they stroll on a secluded beach, and for those who feel a small island provides the only true respite from our boisterous world ...

Tranquility at Killiecrankie Bay.

The "Joinh" at Zeehan

Lake Mackintosh is a power and recreation base

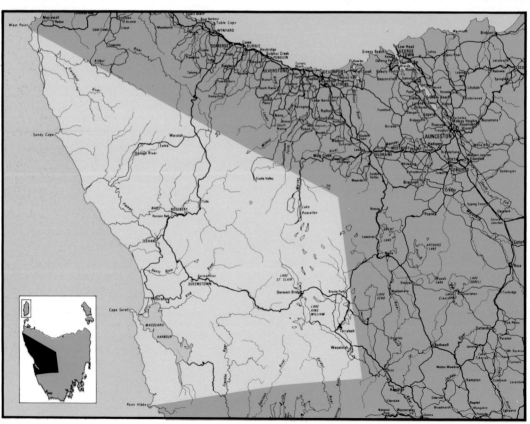

West Coast

Looking at a modern grocery list it is hard to imagine men heading off into the wilds of the West Coast for six months supplied with only flour, two sacks of potatoes, a few sides of bacon and cases of corned beef, baking powder, yeast and sauce to disguise the taste of tainted meat! However these were the rations of the piners and miners, the pioneers of Tasmania's West Coast — a region which extends from the northern bluffs of Cape Grim to the southern fjordlands of Port Davey, and from Hell's Gates at Macquarie Harbour in the west to the Picton River area in the east. The West has had a turbulent history ... almost as rugged as some of its countryside and wind-swept coastline.

In 1815 Captain James Kelly, one of the founders of the whaling industry of Van Diemens Land, discovered and named Port Davey and Macquarie Harbour. The first permanent European settlement was on Sarah Island in Macquarie Harbour in 1822. It was established as a penal settlement that was to become known as the harshest in the colony. Convicts entered the harbour through Hell's Gates — a bitterly apt name for the narrow opening. One of their tasks in this "hell hole on earth" was cutting Huon pine. The value of this timber was recognised as early as 1818 — especially for boat-building.

The penal settlement closed — largely because of the difficult access — but piners continued to seek the "green gold", and in the 1870s miners searched for "yellow gold". Subsequent finds proved that the West is a treasure-trove of minerals — copper, lead, zinc, tin, iron, silver and gold.

![Queenstown, about 1910.]
Queenstown, about 1910.

It was not until 1932 that Queenstown, the largest town on the West Coast, was linked with Hobart by road. The Lyell Highway was known as the West Coast Road, and during its construction families camped along the route. It took three years to build 50 miles of roadway, a fact that can be appreciated when travelling the winding eastern approach to Queenstown.

The modern Murchison Highway links Queenstown with the Waratah Highway, which continues on to Somerset on the North West Coast. Main roads link the highway with other important centres such as Strahan, Zeehan and Savage River. There are coach services six days a week and daily flights by Airlines of Tasmania.

Like the early pioneers we'll head West, travelling the Lyell Highway through the Derwent Valley (see page 19) and on to the highlands, where townships have developed mainly as a result of the hydro electric schemes of the 20th century. Most of the smaller systems are operated by remote control, but stations such as Liapootah, Tarraleah, Tungatina and Trevallyn (in the North) have viewing galleries for visitors.

Tarraleah-Tungatinah power scheme.

Wayatinah — lagoon
Development of the Derwent catchment was one of the first power schemes and Wayatinah, 10 km off the highway and 116 km from Hobart, is the base for personnel operating the six stations of the Lower Derwent system. There is a camping area and limited caravan parking, and the lagoon is good for boating and swimming. The nearby Liapootah control centre can be inspected daily.

Tarraleah — hilltop town
This small township, 122 km from Hobart, is the hilltop home for H.E.C. staff and families, involved with the Tarraleah-Tungatinah power

scheme. It has a shopping centre, heated pool, golf and tennis facilities, camping and caravan areas, a chalet which offers accommodation and meals (book through the H.E.C. in Hobart), and pleasant picnic spots by the highway.

Many of the lakes and lagoons in this region have boat ramps and are a mecca for fishermen. (For details, including Bronte Park, see p.94.) Bradys Lake is a popular venue for white water canoeing, and a world standard course is being developed here.

Bradys Lake is superb for wild water canoeing.

Derwent Bridge — halting spot
During the various stages of the Highway development Derwent Bridge (173 km from Hobart and 83 km from Queenstown) has been regarded as a "stopover". An old hotel used to "revitalise" travellers and now a modern tavern serves a similar role. The tavern is lined with Tasmanian timbers and the travellers can obtain counter meals and relax by the log fires. Food, stores and fuel can be obtained from a roadhouse, and a road leads from here to Lake St Clair at the southern end of the Cradle Mountain, Lake St Clair National Park.

Lake St Clair — wallabies and platypuses
There is a nominal charge for vehicle entry to national parks, fees being used for maintenance work.

Lake St Clair has many attractions — the lake itself (the deepest natural freshwater lake in Australia) and its mountain surrounds, long and short walks, and rich variety of fauna and flora. Picnickers have plenty of company ... wallabies and birds vie for "titbits".

Cabins can be hired from the N.P.W.S. and there are caravan, tent and campervan sites. Camping is allowed in designated area, details of which can be obtained from the ranger. A kiosk has general provisions and souvenirs as well as snacks. The MV **Tequila** provides transport between Cynthia Bay and Narcissus Hut twice daily.

This glacial lake, which is up to 190 metres in depth, is surrounded by majestic mountains, including the State's highest peak, Mt Ossa (1,617 m). Views of the superb reflections are gained on walks along the foreshore — and there may even be a platypus or two.

Inland, waratahs are among flowers lining short walks to places such as Watersmeet, while an 85 km overland track runs through the 126,000 ha park to Cradle Mountain in the north. There are shelters along the way and this is one of the most popular walking tracks in Australia. However, abrupt weather changes are not unusual so walkers should ensure they have adequate equipment and provisions ...

Back on the highway there is barely time to catch breath between the views afforded from the winding sections over Mt Arrowsmith and on the dramatic approach to Queenstown. Tasmania's unique leatherwood honey is produced from the beehives that are placed at various points along the Highway. Beekeepers leave their hives between December and March, when the leatherwood white, waxy flowers appear. Leatherwood originally was called salvewood because a sticky substance which adheres to young growth was found to be useful in healing cuts. About 631 tonnes of the clear, smooth honey are produced each year for Australian consumption and for export to places such as Europe and the U.S.A.

South of the highway about 50 km east of Queenstown is the Franklin-Lower Gordon Wild Rivers National Park. (see p.86). On the approach to Queenstown there are massive mountain peaks as far as the eye can see. Delightful picnic grounds are found near the King River and just out of Queenstown are the old mining towns of Linda and Gormanston. The ruins of Linda, now almost abandoned, stand in an area once alive with sounds of hotels and the bustle of mining. Gormanston is now a satellite residential centre at the foot of Mt Owen.

Scars heal over
For years a stark bareness was a characteristic of the hills around Queenstown. The vegetation was denuded by a combination of rain (the area has Tasmania's highest rainfall), mining, timber cutting and bushfires. Now, however, the regrowth is beginning to reclaim the "moonscape"

Queenstown — mining "through and through"
There is no escaping the fact this is a mining town. Queenstown still retains the atmosphere of the old mining days and undoubtedly is the "capital" of the West. The Mt Lyell Company dominates the town's economy and most residents work in areas connected with company operations.

Although gold had been discovered as early as 1856, it was development of the Iron Blow which led to growth of the Mt Lyell Mining and Railway Company. Gold was worked for about 10 years at Iron Blow, but it was soon replaced by copper as the most profitable mineral. American Robert Sticht produced the first copper from his smelter in 1896 and went on to become manager of the company.

At the turn of the century Queenstown had a population of 5,000 (who made the most of the 14 hotels!) and it was Tasmania's third biggest town.

Fluctuations in world copper prices have been reflected in the changing fortunes of Queenstown. It has also experienced a number of tragedies, particularly a mine disaster in 1912, a fire which ravaged the first town, and a Spanish 'flu epidemic which killed many people in 1918. The 1912 disaster in the North Lyell mine is believed to have started when a pump motor blew out, igniting a pumphouse lined with King Billy pine. It was more than 230 metres underground and, although some miners escaped in cages, 42 lost their lives.

Records of these events are among an extensive collection of photographs and artifacts at the Gallery Museum at the corner of Driffield and Sticht Streets. It is open daily from 9 a.m. – noon, 2-5 p.m., and 7-9 p.m.

See mine operations
The Mt Lyell Company conducts tours of the mine surface operations, daily at 9.15 a.m. and 4 p.m. Rock specimens and literature are available and visitors can also see a museum with items of mining and general historic interest. Tours start at the Western Arts and Crafts Centre.

The company has been a major producer of copper in Australia for more than 100 years. The mine has yielded over 93 million tonnes of ore. In addition to copper the mine has also produced significant quantities of gold and silver. Copper concentrate is sent by rail to Burnie for shipment to Japan, where it is refined and processed. More than two million tonnes of pyrite also has been recovered and sold for acid-making.

Many towns have disppeared
More than 1,000 photos taken before 1940 can be seen in the Imperial Hotel. They provide a fascinating insight into the comings and goings on the West Coast. At Miners Siding, a restored ABT locomotive sits on a trestle bridge that has an incline representing the steepest gradient on the track between Strahan and Queenstown.

A gallery and craft centre has local copperware, Huon pine woodwork, leatherwork and paintings.

Queenstown has hotels, motels, caravan and camping areas, tearooms, a full range of shops and tourist information centres, including a Tasmanian Travel Centre.

There are superb vistas from the Mount Jukes Road, created during a power development project.

Strahan — port of importance
Strahan's importance has always relied on its situation as a port, on Macquarie Harbour, 41 km from Queenstown.

A Huon pine sawmill at the end of the wharf provides a link with the past — rafts of

Queenstown, the main West Coast centre.

Huon pine were floated here from upstream along the Gordon River where piners cut the logs from the forests. In those days the pine was sent from Strahan in log form. Now it is mainly a craft timber and the logs are milled at Strahan.

George Smith, who spent years searching out stands of Huon Pine, is one of the most colourful characters of the West Coast. He has been a letter carrier in Hobart and Strahan, a fisherman in Bass Strait, skipper of a motor launch which carried vegetables weekly from Strahan to Queenstown, a contractor for horse teams collecting pine, and manager of a mill complex. George (who was born in 1900) has provided one of the last first-hand accounts of the pining industry at a time when the timber was used for everything from boats to coffins!

During the 1920s a base camp by the Gordon River would be home for George for stretches of up to 26 weeks. He would take up supplies by boat to Gould's Landing then walk his horses inland. Having cut a track through the bush by the river the hinterland buttongrass plains were easy to cross. Horses pulled timber back to the river and the logs were lashed into rafts for the trip to Strahan. Sometimes George lost logs in tributaries; if floods were late coming he would have already moved on. Generally though, the piners were able to keep an eye on their timber. He said there were never whole forests of Huon Pine — it was always in patches among other species of timber.

Camps, stables and log-loading landings were located at many points along the banks of the Lower Gordon, but fires (including a major one in 1934) have destroyed most of them. At one stage a track was cut from Port Davey to Strahan because of the large number of shipwrecked seamen stranded in the South West, but by 1928 this too, was impassable. About 40 piners were working in the lower reaches of the Gordon when George was there, and in the 1930s a renewed demand for Huon pine encouraged contractors to move upstream above the rapids. During the next 20 years Huon pine was logged from as far as the Olga River.

George set his sights in other directions, however, and in 1940 he moved to Zeehan and became manager of a milling complex until his retirement ...

Most of the timber buildings in Strahan have not stood the test of time, but the old Customs House and Post Office are still prominent on the waterfront esplanade.

Harbour and river cruises

Light planes use Strahan Airport and Wilderness Air conducts seaplane flights over West Coast towns and national parks. However, the most famous passenger conveyors are the Gordon River cruise vessels, which make half and full-day trips on the Gordon River, Australia's deepest river. Cruise schedules should be checked as they vary during the year. Bookings are essential. There are trips upstream to Lime Kiln Reach and to rainforests at Sir John Falls, with its ancient Huon pines. On Macquarie Harbour, points of interest include Hell's Gates, Kelly's Basin and Sarah Island (known as Settlement Island). This isolated island outpost is now maintained by the National Parks and Wildlife Service.

Strahan is on picturesque Macquarie Harbour.

Sarah Island — a dreaded place

The first penal station on Van Diemen's Land was sited at Sarah Island. Such settlements were used as places of punishment for convicts who comitted additional offences. The area is featured in Marcus Clark's famous novel, **For the Term of his Natural Life**, which has also been made into a film and a TV series. The first convicts arrived in 1822 and it became known as the harshest penal settlement in Australia. The lash was not spared and few escapees lived to tell the tale. Rough seas and the narrow entrance to the harbour (which has claimed many victims over the years) made it difficult to get supplies to the island so, in 1834, it was decided to abandon the settlement.

Strahan has a full range of accommodation, including beachside camping grounds. Information on south-western and world heritage areas is available on weekdays in the old Customs Building, while the former Strahan headquarters of the Wilderness Society now houses crafts and the Royal Bank of Avram, with its own currency.

It is worth calling to see the extensive mineral and gemstone collection. Other places of interest include People's Park and Hogarth Falls.

At Ocean Beach, 6 km from Strahan, the surf rolls in from the Southern Ocean, leaving legacies of shell and driftwood. Forty kilometres of huge sand dunes line the shore, while out to sea fishing boats and petroleum exploration teams draw on the resources of an ocean which stretches from here to South Africa ...

Travelling north from Queenstown on the Murchison Highway there is a glacial reserve on the way to Zeehan.

Zeehan — fires force changes

Discovery of rich silver-lead deposits in Zeehan in 1882 changed the face of the small settlement 38 km north of Queenstown. Businesses boomed, 26 hotels did a roaring trade and a stock exchange flourished. In the 1890s it was not uncommon for a dozen new mining companies to be listed on the Tasmanian exchanges in a month. (For half a century shares in Mt Bischoff Tin sold for as high as £100 each — equivalent to $2,000 today).

Mt Zeehan and Mt Heemskirk are named after the two ships in Abel Tasman's 1642 expedition. These West Coast mountains were his first sight of Van Diemen's Land.

Ore worth more than $8 million was produced at Zeehan mines, but then they began to fail and after 1908 the population (then about 10,000) started to decline. Nowadays it has regained its importance because of re-opening of the tin mine at Renison Bell; most of the workers live in Zeehan and travel to work.

The town has had a chequered history and in 1981 many homes were destroyed in bushfires which swept the area. Since then there has been a massive re-building programme and residents have tackled the problems with the same spirit adopted by their pioneer forebears.

Famous museum

Buildings such as the Old Grand Hotel (now flats), the Gaiety Theatre, (where stars such as Dame Nellie Melba held the spotlight) and historic commercial establishments survived the holocaust. So did the School of Mines established in 1894 and now the West Coast Pioneers' Memorial Museum. The museum has displays of equipment from the old Spray Shaft, share certificates, minerals (including crocoite, found in only three places in the world), Tasmanian birds and animals, artifacts of Tasmanian Aborigines, and a mine diorama which shows details of underground workings.

The museum is open daily (except Christmas Day and Good Friday) and its mineral collection is regarded as one of the finest in the world. Refreshments and souvenirs are available and outside children love to clamber over old steam engines and railway carriages. The famous ABT locomotives and the Daimler rail car are of particular interest.

Zeehan has hotels, a motel, caravan park and camping area, an art gallery and craft centre, and tourist information is readily available. Zeehan is set for survival ...

Secondary roads lead to Dundas (now

An ore dresser at Zeehan's Pioneers Memorial Museum.

reclaimed by the bush) and Trial Harbour (a fishing area 23 km out to the coast). New roads lead north to the Pieman hydro-electric scheme, and south to Strahan, on a former railway link.

Renison Bell — renewed activity
The highway passes near the large concentrating mill of this tin mining township, which has had a new lease of life in recent years. There is a hotel at Renison Bell, but most commercial activities are based at Zeehan or Rosebery, 11 km away.

Rosebery — "buckets above"
Ore from the Hercules Mine at Williamsford used to be carried to Rosebery in a series of buckets on an aerial ropeway; at one point it crosses the highway.

Rosebery is a company town; it depends on the Electrolytic Zinc Company. The processing plant can be inspected by arrangement, and Rosebery has a hotel, caravan park with on-site vans, shops, golf, swimming and tennis facilities. Late last century the town grew around a gold mine, but now it is a base for one of the State's newest commercial enterprises — trout fishing tours. Tasmania has a Professional Trout Fishing Guide Association, and one of its members operates from Rosebery. There are four-wheel drive trips to leading fishing areas, and a modern van has accommodation for up to 15 people (and a shower!). All equipment is provided and details can be obtained from Tasmanian Travel Centre.

Pieman River power development
Massive Hydro Electric Commission projects are under way in this area. The Pieman River power development ultimately will have five dams and three power stations, adding more than 20% to the State's total electricity generating capacity. Initial stages involved the construction of a dam and power station at Lake Mackintosh (not open to visitors) and a second station, Bastyan, on Lake Rosebery. The storage at Lake Mackintosh is supplemented by water which comes via a tunnel from the nearby Lake Murchison.

Lake Mackintosh has launching ramps, and fishing and boating are popular. Lake Rosebery, created by the Bastyan Dam on the Pieman River, also is ideal for recreational and sporting activities.

Tullah — new life
Tullah, once a mining town, is now a base for H.E.C. construction workers, and a 55 km road runs from here to the Lower Pieman damsite. There is an H.E.C. tourist information centre at Tullah. A steam engine, Wee Georgie Wood, carries passengers during Summer. A sealed road just north of Tullah leads to the lower Pieman. Motorists can drive across the Reece Dam and back to Zeehan. North of Rosebery the Murchison Highway crosses the Que River, site of massive new zinc and gold developments by Aberfoyle Ltd, south east of Waratah.

Waratah — mine building boom
Construction of houses in Waratah for workers employed on the Que River mining project has given a boost to this township, 117 km from Queenstown and 77 km from Burnie.

Waratah once again is enjoying a period of activity, but it is unlikely that it will reach the peak of late last century when the local Mt Bischoff Mine was the world's richest tin mine. Discovered by James (Philosopher) Smith in 1871 the mine was worked for 50 years, and was the first industrial plant in Australia lit with electricity.

There is good trout fishing in the extensive dam system which formed part of the now-ruined mine complex.

It is presumed that Waratahs were growing here when it was explored by surveyors from the Van Diemen's Land Company — hence the town's name.

Bed and breakfast or full board are available at the Waratah Hotel, and the town has camping and caravan facilities, a picnic and barbecue area and nine-hole golf course.

The Murchison and Waratah Highways merge here, but a secondary road leads west to Corinna and the Pieman River.

Luina — tin mine base
Until 1986, Australia's second largest tin mine was at Mt Cleveland, 16 km from Waratah. Now, the activity is centred on zinc-lead-silver mining at the Hellyer Mine, also near Waratah.

Mt Cleveland has numerous tracks for bushwalking and just past Luina the road crosses the Heazlewood River, which is idea for swimming, fishing and picnics by the foreshore.

Nineteen Mile Camp, a staging post for weary miners in times gone by, now lives on in name only, but Savage River 38 km from Waratah, has earned itself a place on the map.

Savage River — gold to iron ore
Improvements in methods of extracting and treating iron ore has led to recent commercial iron ore developments at Savage River, although deposits were found here as far back as 1877. In those days it was the scene of gold-sluicing operations, prospectors having worked their way through the bush from Corinna.

Construction of the iron ore mining complex in the late 1960s involved American, Australian and Japanese companies. Visitors can see the open-cut mine and associated workings during tours at 9 a.m. and 2 p.m. each Tuesday and Thursday (no children under 12 and women must wear slacks and flat-heeled shoes). Before shipment, the ore is pelletised at Port Latta, 85 km away on the North West Coast. Finely-crushed ore is mixed with water at Savage River to form a slurry, and this is then pumped along a pipeline which connects the two centres.

Savage River is a self-contained township with a hospital, stores and motel (including a licensed restaurant).

Corinna — cruises from here

A gravel road leads to Corinna, 28 km from Savage River. It is on the banks of the Pieman River. Fact has become entwined with fiction in relation to the origin of the river's name. Pieman Alexander Pearce often is credited as being the person after whom the Pieman was named, but official records show the title was derived from pieman Tommy Kent, a pastrycook by trade. "Little Tommy" Kent crossed the river and eventually reached the North-West Coast after absconding from Macquarie Harbour. He was the first European to make this journey.

It was a remarkable feat of endurance for Tommy, who was only 4 ft 11 inches. After being returned to Macquarie Harbour he escaped a second time, heading South on this occasion. Tommy was recaptured at Bathurst Harbour. During his escapes he traversed the whole West Coast on foot.

Fish are plentiful in the river and shacks can be hired. A launch, the **Arcadia II**, makes regular trips on the Pieman, past banks lined with eucalypts, rainforest, ferns and even Huon pine. It is possible to see pine markers on riverside graves as the boat travels to the Pieman Heads, where a stop is made for lunch (take your own). The trip lasts four hours and bookings should be made in advance with Tasbureau or the Savage River Motor Inn where schedule details are available.

Tigers lurked here

Corinna is an Aboriginal word meaning Tasmanian tiger, and this was certainly tiger country. There have been no confirmed sightings of the thylacine (tiger) for more than 50 years, although there have been many unconfirmed reports. Named because of the stripes on its lower back, it is known also as the Tasmanian wolf.

In the early days of white settlement, tigers were such a menace to livestock that a bounty was paid for each one killed. Now it is a protected species, the last known Tasmanian tiger dying in the Hobart Zoo in the 1930s. In subsequent years there have been a number of organised searches, some of them using sophisticated camera equipment, but the tigers (if they exist) still manage to elude the hunters. It is hard to believe that a species which was considered a pest just 100 years ago could have disappeared completely, and researchers hope the wilderness areas may reveal evidence that shows Tasmanian tigers are still "on the move"

The rugged mountain ranges give way abruptly to forests, plains and rich farmlands of the North West. There have been distinctive differences in the development of Tasmanian regions, governed to a large extent by these changes in topography. But it seems that people of the West always will "pull through", despite the changes in fortune which the area experiences.

A Tasmanian tiger.

HUON PINE

Huon pine is found only in Tasmania, although a similar timber once grew in Chile. Favoured by ship builders, cabinet makers and other craftsmen, it is noted for its durability. The wood has a distinctive smell which is produced by its oil that also contributes to its non-decaying quality. Its name was derived from the Huon area where it was first found and the colonial piners referred to it as "green gold".

Today there is limited access to stands of Huon pine, but on the Denison River 30 km from Strathgordan — the Truchanas Reserve contains a remnant stand of one thousand year old Huon pines.

A wide range of crafts made from the timber is available throughout the State — packets of shavings (a reminder, perhaps, of the practice of early settlers of lining furniture with Huon pine to keep out insects) dining room tables, bowls and ornaments.

The best quality timber comes from the West Coast, as rocky areas produce harder, more closely-grained wood. Re-afforestation is impractical because Huon pine grows very slowly. It take up to 800 years to reach 60 cm in diameter, and some trees found during the past century are more than 2,500 years old.

For generations it was prized as a timber for ship building, but present-day economics make it impractical for anything other than occasional use in the industry. The value of Huon pine was recognised as far back as 1818 and items made from the timber are still regarded as good investments.

South West

Tasmania's South West has been declared a world heritage area, and, as a result of bitter debates surrounding the announcement, world attention has been focused on the State.

Parties at the centre of the conflict have been conservationists, who believe the ancient region should be left in its present state, and developers — primarily the Hydro Electric Commission — who want to use the massive water resources for power generation.

Tasmania has more land in national parks than any other Australian State, and the South West includes the Wild Rivers National Park (incorporating the headwaters and rivers of the Franklin and Olga Rivers and part of the Lower Gordon River catchment) and the South West National Park (extending from Lake Pedder to Bathurst Harbour and Port Davey).

Despite their different objectives, both conservationists and developers have added to the tourism potential of the South West. The widespread publicity has resulted in people travelling from many parts of the world to experience this unique wilderness, while the development of hydro schemes, such as the new Lake Pedder, are among Tasmania's major tourist attractions.

Ancient pre-Cambrian rocks underlie most of the central South West and some of the vegetation resembles that found in Chile and New Zealand. The climate is harsh, shelters and cleared tracks are few — careful planning is therefore vital, especially in relation to equipment and provisions.

The Wild Rivers National Park has dramatic canoeing and rafting waters, but again, the necessity for care and experience cannot be stressed too strongly.

Port Davey was discovered and named by whaler-explorer Captain James Kelly in 1815, and the area has seen its share of whalers and fishermen over the years.

Only a handful of people have made their permanent home in the region, the veteran of them all is Denny King. He first went there in 1930 with his father who prospected for tin at Cox Bight. Denny grew up in the Huon, but after World War II moved permanently to Melaleuca Inlet, his only trips to Hobart in those days being annual expeditions for supplies and to deliver tin mined on his property. He has three leases in a corridor of land open for mining between Bathurst Harbour and Cox Bight. The only other permanent residents — members of the Wilson family — have an adjoining lease.

Denny radios out every day and gives weather reports for the Bureau of Meteorology, but there have been times when he has been completely isolated. Regular visitors include his daughters, Janet and Mary, who in the 1950s, were the first Tasmanians to participate in the South Australian based radio School of the air.

Surveying the scene at Port Davey, circa 1890's.

Denny has found plenty of evidence of earlier visitors — both black and white. There are Aboriginal middens, flints and throwing stones; chimneys and mounds of moss and stone, where piners lived at Spring River; stone fireplaces and other relics of the whaling days at Bramble Cove.

During the past 35 years Denny has assisted many bushwalkers, fishermen and other visitors to the area. In the mid 1950s he built a 1,000 foot airstrip, which later was extended and bought by the Government. In summer months, there are frequent daily flights. The practice of dropping supplies from the air for walkers has been stopped because of litter problems, but provisions can be flown in at Cox Bight or Melaleuca Inlet and stored in a hut built by the N.P.W.S. The costs of building the hut were covered by money given in memory of a walker who lost his life in the area. After the winter months, when Denny and other "permanents" may go for many weeks without seeing anyone, the arrival of visitors is quite a novelty. In recent times he has met more people from interstate and overseas, but said the only change which has resulted from an increased number of visitors is that tracks are more clearly visible ...

A round trip
The traditional walk in the South West is between Port Davey or Cox Bight and Cockle Creek near Recherche Bay. Vehicles can be driven to Cockle Creek and the walk takes up to 10 days. Light planes from Cambridge are available for flights in or out of the South West (and for scenic tours of the area). There are also numerous escorted wilderness tours, some of which combine flying and hiking. Food and equipment are provided, and details can be obtained from Tasmanian Travel Centre

Sunset at Lake Pedder.

The South West encompasses mountain ranges, glacial lakes, beaches and buttongrass plains. Its strength lies in its wilderness, and anyone entering the area should remember it is not a power to be tackled lightly.

The ranger in the South West National Park is at Maydena (reached via the Derwent Valley), the starting point for the 85 km Gordon Road leading to Strathgordon, 159 km from Hobart. A nominal charge is made for use of the road, which was carved out of some of Australia's most forbidding terrain.

Strathgordon — "power base"
A township constructed to house workers employed on the H.E.C. Gordon-Pedder power projects, Strathgordon is the main centre for people visiting Lake Pedder, the Gordon Dam and power station. Wood, electric barbecues,

and shelters, are provided at several points along the access route, and there is a lookout on a secondary road to the Scotts Peak and Edgar Dam sites. Camping areas have been developed at Edgar Dam, Scotts Peak and Ted's Beach.

The number of permanent residents in Strathgordon is declining, but an increasing number of people are using the town as a holiday, recreation and fishing resort. There are camping and caravan areas, but the main accommodation complex is a chalet which formerly housed H.E.C. personnel. The Lake Pedder Chalet has motel accommodation (with a special emphasis on family requirements), and a licensed dining room which is open to the public.

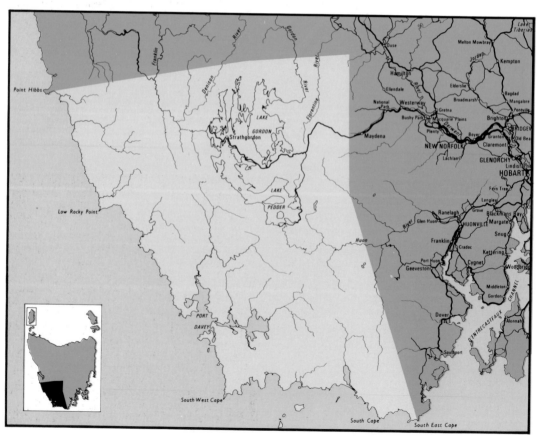

South-west rainforest.

Lake Pedder

Together, Lake Pedder and nearby Lake Gordon cover more than 500 square kilometres and hold 27 times the volume of water in Sydney Harbour; they form Australia's largest freshwater storage.

Boating facilities cater for people who want to travel on Lake Pedder or try their luck in catching some of the massive trout for which the region has become famous. Boat launching areas have been developed and Lake Pedder is a fisherman's paradise. There are regular tales of 12 kg trout that **didn't** get away!

Walk either way

A track starting near Scott's Peak Dam leads to Port Davey and the south coast, through the South West National Park — the largest in the State. Wombats, pademelons and wallabies can be seen in the area, and this is the habitat of the rare orange-bellied parrot and the more common green ground parrots and honeyeaters.

A track off the Scott's Peak Road leads to Mt Eliza (one-day return trip) and Mt Anne (overnight camp necessary).

Gordon Dam — majestic

The Gordon Dam site is spectacular, both at the dam itself and deep underground in the power station. Information is available at a visitors' centre perched high above the dam. Bookings can be made here for a somewhat unusual bus ride. Trips are made daily between 10.45 a.m. and 3.30 p.m. (except Christmas Day and Good Friday) through a tunnel, to view operation of the station and exhibits relating to its development. Those with a head for heights can walk across the dam, and a cable car travels 150 m down the reverse side of the dam into the Gordon Gorge.

Gordon power station.

The South-West is true wilderness.

The trip to Strathgordon can be made in a day from Hobart, but with the increasing range of attractions in the area it is worth at least an overnight stay.

Wild Rivers National Park

This is one of Tasmania's new national parks, and incorporates earlier reserves at Frenchman's Cap and the Gordon River, and the Truchanas Nature Reserve with its stand of mature Huon pine trees.

It was the debate about the future of the wild Franklin River and its associated features that has caused so much interest in the area. Among these features are caves with evidence of habitation by Ice Age man. With the end of the Ice Age rainforest enveloped the caves, preventing further human contact for 15,000 years. The caves were re-discovered during recent exploration and thousands of Aboriginal relics have been recovered from the Kutikina and DeenaReena Caves.

Some choose walks ...

There are various walks in the park, ranging from a short trip to Donaghy's Hill from the Lyell Highway for a view of Frenchman's Cap and the Franklin River, to walks of several days duration into the Irenabyss and Frenchman's Cap (a quartzite peak with a 300 m face on the eastern side). The track to the Cap passes over buttongrass and through rainforests which includes stands of King Billy pine.

... others prefer rafts and canoes

People planning rafting or canoeing trips on the Franklin River during Summer months must be well experienced. The river has no respect for life, and if trips have to be abandoned the only way out is via the Fincham Track (a full days walk) or the Mt McCall four-wheel drive H.E.C. track (involving up to two days walking). Rafters and canoeists start their journey at the Collingwood River Bridge on the Lyell Highway, 200 km from Hobart and 40 km from Queenstown. The average party takes 14 days to reach the point on the Lower Gordon where cruise vessels pick up rafters, by prior arrangement. However, an extra week's rations should be taken in case floods cause delays and parties should not exceed six people. Advice on all aspects of bushwalking and other national park activities can be obtained from walking clubs, the Tasmanian Wilderness Society and the N.P.W.S. pamphlets about water safety on the wild rivers are produced by the Tasmania Police ... they have a vested interest as they are involved in numerous rescues and searches.

The most spectacular section of the river is the Great Ravine, with its four main rapids — aptly named The Churn, Coruscades, Thunderush and Cauldron.

These **are** wild regions and should be treated with due respect.

The Franklin River still runs free.

Midlands and Central Highlands

The road between Launceston and Hobart was established as a cart track and stock route long before coaches embarked on the road in 1832. Settlers had travelled between the two centres as early as 1807. Villages and inns were soon established at many points along the road which later became a favourite haunt for bushrangers. Now the Midland Highway is Tasmania's major road. Its course has changed during the past decade and now many of the historic towns are by-passed, but it is worth detouring to see them. Melton Mowbray is at the highway's junction with the Lake Highway which leads to Bothwell and the mountains and lakes of the Central Highlands.

Franklin Village, 6 km from Launceston, is the first stop when travelling south on the Midland Highway. Franklin House, an 1838 Georgian style property, was the first bought by the National Trust's Tasmanian branch. It was built for Launceston brewer and innkeeper Britton Jones, and from 1852 to 1867 was a boys' school. It is open daily for inspection, except from 12.30 to 1.30 pm. and on Christmas Day and Good Friday.

Recycled "watering hole"

The 1839 Woolpack Inn is typical of colonial inns offering 20th century travellers refreshments of a different kind. It now has tearooms and a museum featuring historic photography and a gallery with displays of work by Tasmanian artists. A deviation at Breadalbane (once called Brumby's Plains) via Western Junction (site of Launceston's airport) leads to historic Evandale. There are donkey trail rides at Breadalbane, and a host farm which has accommodation for four non-smokers!

Shearers gather for work, circa 1880's.

Evandale — like an English village

Settlers from Norfolk Island came to Evandale in 1816 and they soon recognised its worth as a farming area.

The village atmosphere has been retained and Evandale has a rich heritage of buildings. Waterloo veteran John Whitehead donated £1 per foot in height of the spire at St Andrew's Church, erected in 1871. Original shopfronts, such as those of Village Antiques and the old Butchery, add a charming touch.

There are old inns, including the 1836 Prince of Wales and the delightfully refurbished Clarendon Arms (both with meals and accommodation), a Colonial Art Gallery specialising in works by early and contemporary Tasmanian artists, antique and craft outlets. The Sunday market is like a village gathering of bygone times.

In recent years the township has become

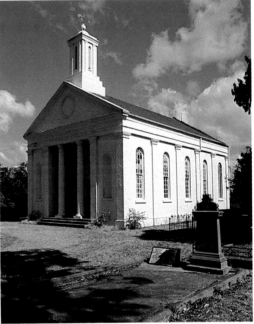

St Andrews Church, Evandale.

synonymous with the annual Penny Farthing Championships. Competitors travel thousands of kilometres to compete in races around the town centre. The event is the highlight of Evandale's Village Festival, a celebration that is accompanied by a return to colonial costumes and all the fun of the fair. Famous past residents of the district include artists John Glover and Tom Roberts; John Batman, Melbourne's founder, who lived south of Evandale for 15 years; and convict "Red" Kelly, father of the famous Ned Kelly, who worked on a local property.

for 15 years; and convict "Red" Kelly, father of the famous Ned Kelly, who worked on a local property.

Grandeur on a large scale
A National Trust property, Clarendon, is 8 km from Evandale. One of Australia's finest Georgian residences, it was built in 1838 for James Cox, a landowner, merchant and Legislative Councillor. The main house is open for inspection daily (except for Christmas Day, Good Friday, and during July). In addition there are two brick service wings with displays which give an insight into how "the other half" lived. It is also pleasant to stroll in the extensive gardens, and there are picnic, playground and barbecue areas.

Deddington — quaint chapel
Artist John Glover left his mark here in more ways than one. He named the area in 1830 after a village in which he had lived in England, and it is believed he designed the simple chapel built in 1842. It has been restored by the National Trust and Glover is buried in the nearby cemetery ...

South of Breadalbane on the Midland Highway is Perth, 18 km from Launceston.

Inns and churches
If the number of inns indicates the popularity of old coaching stops, Perth must have been near the top of the list. The Leather Bottell Inn is now a restaurant specialising in French provincial cuisine, and there are also the Jolly Farmer and Old Crown Inns. By contrast, there are several churches, including the octagonal Baptist Tabernacle (1889).

A handy spot for stocking up on petrol and crafts, Perth also has delightful riverside picnic grounds, and just south of the town is the Symons Plains motor racing circuit.

A road leads from Perth to Longford and Cressy, rich agricultural districts ...

Clarendon, a National Trust property.

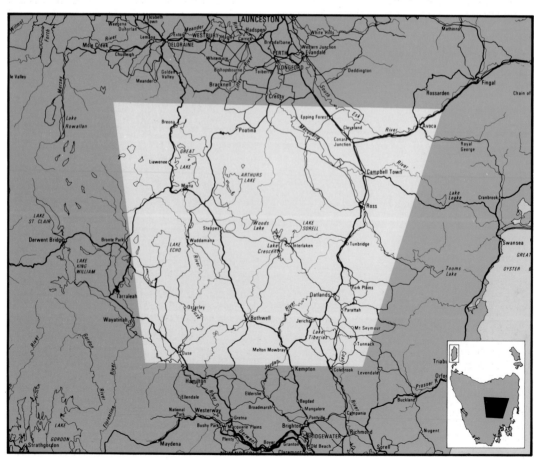

Longford — history from mills to mansions

This once was a major wheat growing area for Port Jackson and Port Phillip. Flour milling was an important industry in the colonial days. A four storey mill in Union Street now is used as a produce store, while remnants of other mills dot the township. The area was known for many years as Norfolk Plains because of the large number of settlers who came from Norfolk Island.

The oldest public building in Longford is Toll House in Wellington Street and nearby, the Longford Library, with a large gas lamp over its entrance, operates in the former Tattersalls Hotel. Imposing Christ Church, built by convicts in 1839, is noted for its windows and clock. The west window is regarded as one of the finest in Australia.

Longford has hotel accommodation, camping and caravan areas, restaurants and shops. This is a good place for buying antiques. Tasmania has long been regarded as a prime "hunting ground" for items from the colonial days.

Brickendon, a Georgian style home, is open daily for visitors who can view the grounds, some rooms and a museum. There are also a coach house, cottage, barns and chapel. The property is owned by descendants of the original owner, William Archer.

There is a touch of England in Longford's many hawthorn-lined roads.

Deer and native animals

The Longford Wildlife Park and picnic area is along Pateena Road on part of a property, Mount Ireh, which was granted to Captain Edward Dumaresq in 1824 and still is farmed by his descendants. Fallow deer roam the area along with Forester kangaroo, Rufus and Bennetts wallabies, Cape Barren geese and occasional nocturnal marsupials. A road winds through the park, and a walk along some of the tracks give the chance to study native flora. Barbecues and firewood are provided.

Cressy — rural emphasis

An important farming area, Cressy was named for the Cressy Company, one of the British groups involved in exploration of Van Diemen's Land. Poppies are now an important crop in the area; the poppy oil is used in making codeine. Tasmania is the only Australian State where there is licensed oil poppy production ...

Midland changes

Epping Forest, 45 km from Launceston, was named by Governor Macquarie who found the then uncleared region reminiscent of Epping Forest in England.

Cleveland, a further 6 km south, was a coaching stop and a depot for ticket-of-leave convicts. Ironically, three of the few buildings still standing were all inns — the Squeaker, the Bald Faced Stag and St Andrew's Inn, which has served as a restaurant in more recent times.

Conara Junction was known originally as The Corners and was a station for passengers changing trains to travel to St Marys on the East Coast. Now only freight trains are travelling the tracks. The highway no longer passes through

Christ Church at Longford.

Conara, but there is a picnic area by the roadside.

Campbell Town — old garrison

This was a garrison town between Hobart and Launceston, but now it is the centre of an important wool growing district. Georgian, Gothic revival and Victorian buildings are scattered through Campbell Town which was named by Governor Macquarie after his wife's maiden name. She was called Elizabeth and Campbell Town is on the Elizabeth River. The bridge over the river was built in 1838 and nearby is the Masonic Lodge, formerly a brewery. The 1840 Grange, owned by the National Trust, is the venue for residential schools run by the Adult Education Department. St Andrew's Presbyterian Church contains an organ and desk which belonged to Bishop Nixon, Tasmania's first Anglican Bishop. A memorial commemorates the achievements of Harold Gatty who was born in Campbell Town in 1931 and later was the navigator with an American adventurer on the first flight around the world. Gatty founded Fiji Airways, the forerunner of Air Pacific.

A secondary road leads from Campbell Town to Lake Leake and on to Swansea on the East Coast ...

Campbell Town's bridge was built by convicts in the 1830's.

This is a good spot for bushwalkers and fishermen. Boats can be hired and there is a boat ramp and picnic and barbecue areas at the lake. The Laird O'Lake Leake Hotel has accommodation for 12 people ...

Ross — historic "gem"
A short distance off the Midland Highway, Ross (81 km from Launceston and 121 km from Hobart) is famous for its superfine wool which has brought world record prices. It is a classified historic town and was one of the earliest settlements; it has served as a military post, coach change and stock market.

The best-known feature of Ross is its bridge; the third oldest in Australia, but architecturally, the most important. Convicts Daniel Herbert and James Colbeck were responsible for the intricate workmanship, Herbert carving the 186 panels which decorate the arches. Details can be studied through binoculars mounted near the bridge. Herbert's tomb is among those in the old military burial ground, where headstone inscriptions make fascinating reading.

The Man O' Ross Hotel opened its doors in 1817, but was rebuilt in 1831 and panelled in Tasmanian oak.

Buildings "tell tales"
The Scotch Thistle Inn has had a varied life —inn, store, midwifery centre, private home, and now a licensed restaurant. The adjacent barn and stables with their original floor and some of the old fittings also are worth a visit.

The Old Barracks, restored by the National Trust, are near the town centre with its four corners representing Temptation (Man O'Ross Hotel), Recreation (Town Hall), Salvation (church) and Damnation (old gaol).

A highlight of the year is the Ross Rodeo at the beginning of November when riders travel from near and far to show their skills.

Facilities include a tourist information centre in the Village Tearooms, a location map

Historic buildings abound in Ross.

Ross Bridge is noted for its carvings.

and recorded commentary outside the Town Hall, shops, hotel accommodation, and a council camping and caravan park with holiday cabins. The town has an extensive museum collection of militaria.

Ross is a good base for trout fishing at Lakes Sorell, Crescent and Tooms, all within an hour's travel.

Wool production history

Displays in the new Tasmanian Wool Centre outline the history of wool production in the Tasmanian Midlands and the development of the Ross district, in general. The Australian Wool Corporation and the Fuji Keori Company of Japan, which has paid top world prices for Tasmanian wool, are among exhibitors. Tasmanian arts and crafts are available for sale. The centre is open daily.

Tunbridge — see the Royal Mail

The township, formerly called Tunbridge Wells, is now just off the highway, but buildings carry reminders of the days when it was the central stopover for coaches.

The Victoria Inn still has sandstone coaching steps, stables adjoin the Tunbridge Wells Inn, and a restored Royal Mail coach forms an appropriate coaching monument. No doubt convicts were pleased to leave behind a relic

A Royal Mail coach at Tunbridge.

of their road building works — a roller shaped from a single block of stone!

Hot air currents at Woodbury, (just south of Tunbridge), favour gliding and skydiving, and clubs meet regularly at weekends. In recent times the massive shale deposit in the Woodbury area have been explored as a possible source of oil.

Antill Ponds — virtually halfway

Only broken walls stand where the old Halfway House signalled a welcome stopping place for travellers. But stonework from the hotel has been incorporated in shelters and a toilet block at a pretty rest area. Coin-operated barbecues are also available. Along the highway there are a few examples of the work of a topiarist who shaped trains, rams and emus out of roadside bushes. They make an interesting diversion for children.

Oatlands — wealth of Georgian structures

Most of the buildings here were erected in the first half of the 19th century and Oatlands (84 km from Hobart, 117 km from Launceston) has the largest collection of Georgian architectural styles in Australia.

In the 1820s Oatlands was one of four military posts along the main road and in the boom days of the 1830s, churches, schools, houses, hotels and community centres were built in the town. Life revolved around military operations and the local industries such as brewing and milling.

The Callington Mill and its associated buildings now are assuming some of their past glory — thanks to restoration work of the N.P.W.S. and the National Trust. The Trust owns the old Supreme Courthouse established in 1829. The Courthouse is on the shores of Lake Dulverton, now a wildlife sanctuary and popular recreation and picnic area.

Oatlands has several antique and craft shops. There is a National Trust giftshop, tearooms,

The Callington Mill is being restored at Oatlands.

and a delightful BYO restaurant, Holyrood House, which even has a separate dining room for non-smokers. There are two hotels — Colonial accommodation is a feature. Oatlands Lodge, a favourite with many trout fishing enthusiasts, is in High Street. Nearby, there are Forget-me-not and Amelia Cottages, which are part of the Waverley Cottage Collection created by a local pastoralist's wife. Waverley Cottage, on a rural property, was originally a 19th century workman's cottage. Next to it is The Croft, a cottage built from sandstone originally used in an old farm building. Details of the refurbishing in all the cottages have to be seen to be believed. Light fittings, for instance, are made from old skirting boards, a wooden stool once served as a wool press, and lampshades are spun from wool from the farm. Oatlands also has two hotels, a camping ground and a youth hostel.

Jericho — mud walls
Mud bricks are among the more unusual building materials used in modern Tasmanian homes, but at Jericho, just off the highway, there are mud walls which once formed part of a probation station 2 km north of the town centre.

Farm accommodation is available on one of the area's leading properties, Ellesmere, where a self-contained pine-log cabin has accommodation for six people. Activities include bushwalking, tennis, horse riding and swimming. (Turn east at the Jericho crossroads on the highway).

Melton Mowbray — hotel of old
A continuously licensed hotel built in 1849, stands at the junction of the Midland and Lake Highways, and outside the hotel is one of Tasmania's few remaining public horse troughs. It was installed before 1850 and was carved from one piece of stone.

The Lake Highway leads 20 km to Bothwell and into the highlands.

Kempton — interesting churches
A number of Georgian and Victorian buildings are to be found at Kempton just off the highway 46 km north of Hobart. Focal points include the attached brick and stone shops (built in 1833), the Wilmot Arms (a faithfully restored coaching inn with colonial accommodation for 13 people) the Congregational Church (built of sandstone reputed to have come from a ruined English church), and St Mary's Church of England (with its historic churchyard). Kempton has hotels, including colonial accommodation, and numerous craft outlets, such as Tittmouse Cottage.

Just south of here is Bagdad, another area named by Hugh Germaine from one of his favourite books, 'The Arabian Nights. Here there is a pleasant sanctuary and picnic area at Chauncy Vale, reached via a signposted road leading off the highway.

Pontville — source of stone
An historic town 27 km north of Hobart, Pontville has many buildings made of sandstone from the local quarries. The stone is just as keenly sought today as it was last century. The Romanesque style St Mark's Church of England built in 1840, has an interesting graveyard. Other buildings of note are the former post office, originally the officers' mess, and The Row, once the barracks for the military overseers of road building works. The restored Epsom Inn has colonial-style accommodation for five people (with all of today's amenities!), while counter lunches are available at the 1832 Crown Inn.

Nearby is Brighton, a modern-day military base, 24 km from Hobart. It also has several stores, a tavern, and a wildlife centre, Bonorong Park, with barbecue and picnic areas.

Bridgewater — housing development
Originally called Green Point, Bridgewater is on the outskirts of Hobart and now is the site for a large government housing development, with associated facilities and shopping centres.

The causeway across the Derwent River represents one of the State's earliest engineering feats. Convicts in chain gangs carted more than two million tonnes of stone during the 20 years of construction. Black swan are found in large numbers in the Derwent River wildlife sanctuary. Over the causeway and then it is just 18 km to the heart of Hobart ...

The highlands of Tasmania and the highlands of Scotland have much in common. Tasmania, too, has its Lake Country, a plateau ranging from 305 metres above sea level in the Clyde Valley at Bothwell to more than 1,000 metres at the Great Lake.

Highland rivers with their vast quantities of water form the basis for some of the State's massive hydro electric schemes, the first of which came on line in 1916. At the opening, the Governor-General, Sir Ronald Munro-Ferguson, said, "When the good fairy passed over Australia she scattered her choicest gifts, but the water sprite established herself in Tasmania alone, and her cup in the central hills is filled to overflowing, and man has shown that he can keep it full to the brim — a bright day is dawning for Tasmania". They were prophetic words ... especially for trout fishermen who seek the "big ones" in mountain streams and lakes, both natural and man-made.

Travelling on the Lake Highway from Melton Mowbray (54 km from Hobart, 144 km from Launceston) the first town is Bothwell. This was settled by Scottish emigrants as early as 1821. Soon it developed as an important agricultural area and was the district headquarters for the military.

Some of the settlers brought golf clubs with them and the first game in Australia was played at Logan's Links on chipped greens (like tennis courts). Not long afterwards links at Ratho became headquarters of the golfing fraternity.

The ancestors of Mrs Madeline Downie were early settlers in the area who made their mark in the development of the milling and wool industries. Members of her family still are involved with sheep farming in the Bothwell district.

Mrs Downie was born in 1899 and witnessed many changes as horses, bullocks and mattocks were replaced with modern machinery. In those days rabbits were the scourge of farmers, and even trappers — the "rabbiters" — could not handle the vast numbers. According to Mrs Downie the introduction of myxomatosis (a disease which wiped out large numbers of rabbits) saved the day. Now, however, Tasmnian devils are posing problems as they move closer to settlements. Rabbits were one of their main sources of food, and they would even scratch out holes to get at young rabbits.

There have been plenty of highs and lows in the wool industry, but one tradition that has not survived is that of the farmer buying a new

A coach prepares to leave Bothwell.

hat if he topped the wool market! Roads were rough and poorly formed and a trip to Hobart for Mrs Downie as a young girl involved a two and a half hour journey by horse and coach to Apsley, then a further three hours by train to Hobart, where rows of "cabs" waited for fares.

Each year shepherds and stockmen round up animals after summer grazing in the highlands and bring them back to Bothwell and surrounding areas for the winter. This annual grazing cycle was established last century.

Bothwell, itself, remains comparatively unspoilt — the old world aspect of the village proves a special attraction for visitors today. Although it is the service centre for a large agricultural district, it still has more than 50 stone and convict brick buildings of note in the town. St Luke's Uniting Church, designed by John Lee Archer, was originally used by both Presbyterians and Anglicans, and is the oldest Presbyterian church in Australia. Wentworth House, home of Mr and Mrs Downie for many years, was built in 1833 by Captain D'Arcy Wentworth, whose brother William built Sydney's Vaucluse House. The first public library in Tasmania was conducted in Bothwell in 1837 in a building still in use in Alexander Street.

Mill of another era

One of the few water powered mills now in operation has been restored on a property called Thorpe. Most of Tasmania's watermills fell into disrepair when competition from larger steam roller mills made it uneconomical to produce flour with stones and waterwheels. During its 81 years of operation the mill was used to grind wheat grown on the property and on surrounding farms. It is open on request for groups of 12 or more.

The Village and Folk Museum has a collection ranging from war medals and nursery items to vintage cars. It is open by appointment.

Wool and spinning

Wool production is vital to the district so it is appropriate that woollen goods are a speciality at the local craft shop.

Once a year Bothwell becomes the "mecca" for spinning and weaving enthusiasts who travel from all parts of the State to take part in a Highland Spin-In. On this "one day of the year", during winter, Bothwell's school hall is filled with bags of locally-grown wool, spinning wheels and teams of pliers, spinners and knitters who compete for the prestige of producing the best knitted square. These are later made into a rug for an elderly citizen.

Base for fishing trips

A picnic area with gas barbecues is located amid century old elms of Queens Park. The town has food stores, accommodation for 11 people at the historic Castle Hotel and for 14 people at the Crown Fishing Lodge, where a guide is available for fishing trips. Bothwell pioneers introduced trout ova into highland lakes, now renowned for their fishing waters.

Other places of interest in the highlands include Waddamana, on a secondary road 26 km south of Great Lake. An H.E.C. Power Museum is open each weekday and from noon to 2 p.m. at weekends.

Miena, 58 km north of Bothwell was the site of an early H.E.C. project. Family and fishermen's accommodation are available at the Compleat Angler and Great Lake Hotels, plus caravan facilities. Poatina forms the northern gateway to the highlands. Tours of the underground power station leave half-hourly from a visitors' reception centre between 9 a.m. and 4 p.m. daily, except Christmas Day and Good Friday. There's accommodation at the H.E.C. Chalet.

TROUT FISHING

For many years only Tasmanian anglers knew the vagaries of the wily trout and the best places to catch this gamest of freshwater game-fish. But now, thanks to the State's progressive tourism policy, the secret is well and truly out. There are hundreds of lakes and streams teeming with beautiful browns and powerful rainbows.

Fishermen can either "go it alone" or join one of the escorted tours, which provide equipment and transport (details from Tasmanian Travel Centres or the Tasmanian Professional Trout Fishing Guides Association). Accommodation includes hotels at the Great Lake and the Crown Lodge at Bothwell.

Popular spots include Great Lake and Arthurs Lake which are reached by either the Poatina Road or the Lake Highway. A new hotel provides accommodation at the Great Lake.

For the amateur or the experienced, a visit to Lake Sorell is likely to be very productive. This is one of the most popular lakes in the State, and throughout the season from August to April it is frequented by many of the State's top fishermen; they often get their bag limit in a single day's fishing. Extensive camping facilities have been developed on the shores by the Lands Department. During the past few seasons this water produced thousands of fish in one to two kilogram class, with the occasional three and four kilogram catch bagged by fishermen with fly and spinner.

For the four-wheel drive enthusiast who does not mind roughing it, a whole new area is just beginning to become popular. Known as the Western Lakes, this is largely virgin trout territory — very rough going, but a favourite with former Prime Minister Malcolm Fraser.

Central highlands are a mecca for trout fishermen.

The Marlborough Highway in the Central Highlands passes a fly fisherman's paradise, Little Pine Lagoon — recognised as the best fly fishing in Australia. A little farther along is a Bronte Park, a small town in the centre of the Lake Country where a chalet has accommodation for 47 people. This is an ideal location for setting off to favourite spots such as Bronte Lagoon, Laughing Jack Lagoon and Brady's Lake. London Lakes has quality dry fly fishing waters (fee required; up-market accommodation for 10 people).

However, when all others fail to produce a fish, try Lake King William, where fish are plentiful, but a little smaller; average size is half to one kilogram. Do not hesitate to ask for advice on the type of fly or lure to use in the various waters — local knowledge may be the difference between a good and bad day.

Snow often covers the highlands in winter.

Waratahs are among Tasmania's native flora.

CONCLUSION

Tasmania often is described as the Treasure Isle. Set between the Southern Ocean and Tasman Sea it has a wealth of offerings for visitors. You simply have to lift the lid and choose ... enrichment is sure to follow.

Index